106 GRAND CANAL

A SCROLL-SAW JOB IN WHITE AND BROWN

1" SQUARES

106 GRAND CANAL

1511

15"   1" SQUARES

1511

SCROLL-SAWED FROM ¾" PLYWOOD

BROWN STRIPES ON BUFF-WHITE BREAST

THE PARROT LENDS ITSELF TO BRIGHT COLORS

SUGGESTED VARIATIONS FOR THE DESIGN IN PHOTO BELOW

1001

222

$$1\ 2\ 3$$
$$4\ 5\ 6$$
$$7\ 8\ 9\ 0$$

CUT FROM PLYWOOD, PAINTED, AND ATTACHED WITH BRADS, SCREWS

420

CONCRETE BLOCK WITH BLACK NUMERALS AGAINST ALUMINUM PAINT IN RECESSED PANEL

BEVELED

Pat's Place

322

MOLD IS KNOCKED APART TO REMOVE BLOCK

SPELLED-OUT NUMBERS ARE ATTRACTIVE

THE BOY MECHANIC

Best Projects from the Classic Series

Popular Mechanics Company

DOVER PUBLICATIONS, INC.
Mineola, New York

Bibliographical Note

This Dover edition, first published in 2006, is a new selection of projects com-
piled from the 1940 and 1945 editions of *The Boy Mechanic,* originally published
by Popular Mechanics Press, Chicago.

Library of Congress Cataloging-in-Publication Data

The boy mechanic : best projects from the classic series / Popular Mechanics
Company.
    p. cm.
    Selection of articles from the 1940 and 1945 editions of The boy mechanic
published by Popular Mechanics Press, Chicago.
    ISBN-13: 978-0-486-45227-2 (pbk.)
    ISBN-10: 0-486-45227-1 (pbk.)
    1. Handicraft for boys—Juvenile literature. I. Popular mechanics (Chicago,
Ill. : 1959)

TT160.B794 2006
745.5—dc22

        2006047425

Manufactured in the United States by Courier Corporation
45227103   2014
www.doverpublications.com

Projects

Wood Penguin Waddles in Lifelike Manner

Although he's remarkably realistic in color, size and also in his manner of getting about, this penguin is made of wood and is pushed with a stick. Body and head are shaped from one piece of $1\frac{3}{16}$-in. plywood while the wings and legs, or feet, are separate parts cut from $\frac{1}{2}$-in. material and pivoted to the body. The curve of the feet is the important thing as it is this curve which allows the penguin to walk in a lifelike manner. Of course, the feet must be pivoted so that they swing freely. This is done by drilling an oversize hole in each leg for a round-headed screw. A thin washer is placed over the screw between the leg and the body and also under the screw head. The wings can be pivoted in the same way.
—Dick Hutchinson, Ithaca, N. Y.

BIRD HUTS

Colony houses are especially suitable for purple martins

RIDGE ROLL OF COPPER BENT OVER ½" DOWEL

CUT AWAY TO FORM OPENING OVER VENTILATING SHAFT

¼" HOLE FOR VENTILATION

2½" DIA.

VENTILATING SHAFT

½" PINE ROOF

SHEET COPPER

END GABLE

BACK SLOPE ROOF

BACK

ROOF COVERED WITH THIN SHEET COPPER

½" HOLES FOR VENTILATING

VENTILATING SHAFT

A private bungalow for wrens

1" DIA.

COVERED WITH BIRCH BARK

and BIRD HOTELS

Four designs for wrens or bluebirds

HERE are several designs for bird houses that should meet the requirements of almost any lover of birds. Among those shown, are colony houses, four-apartment log cabins and single-apartment homes of rustic design, which are made from short sections of logs. Essential dimensions in building bird houses are the sizes of the nesting compartment and the entrance hole, which are given in the table. For colony houses, use ¾-in. selected cypress or California redwood for durability. Small single-apartment homes, for wrens and bluebirds, may be constructed of lighter material, and require no perch as the birds fly directly into the entrances. The small frame houses and the log-cabin types should be colored with brown or green shingle stain, while white paint, with a harmonizing trim color, is best for colony houses. The latter should be mounted rigidly on a stout post, which is pivoted at the bottom so that they can be lowered for cleaning. Also, note that the colony houses have a built-in system of ventilation, which is essential. The construction of the rustic-bark homes is clearly shown. Those made from single logs are ripped, and, after the cavity has been chiseled out, the halves are fastened together with wire or large screws. A thin coating of asbestos-roofing cement spread on the joining faces of the two halves will keep water out of the nesting cavity.

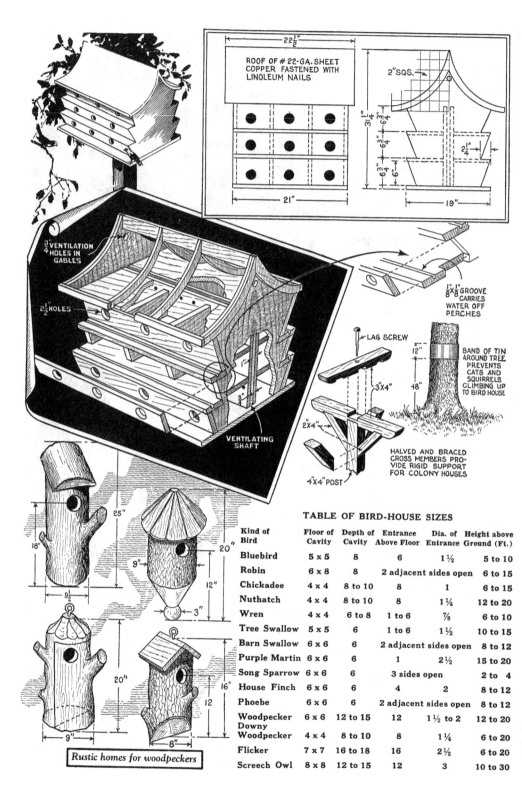

ROOF OF #22-GA. SHEET COPPER FASTENED WITH LINOLEUM NAILS

22½"

21"

2" SQS.

31¼"

6¾" 6¾"

6¾" 6"

2¼"

19"

¾" VENTILATION HOLES IN GABLES

2½" HOLES

1"

VENTILATING SHAFT

⅛"X⅛" GROOVE CARRIES WATER OFF PERCHES

LAG SCREW

3"X4"

2"X4"

4"X4" POST

12"

48"

BAND OF TIN AROUND TREE PREVENTS CATS AND SQUIRRELS CLIMBING UP TO BIRD HOUSE

HALVED AND BRACED CROSS MEMBERS PROVIDE RIGID SUPPORT FOR COLONY HOUSES

25"

18"

9"

9½"

20"

12"

3"

20"

16"

12

9"

8"

Rustic homes for woodpeckers

TABLE OF BIRD-HOUSE SIZES

Kind of Bird	Floor of Cavity	Depth of Cavity	Entrance Above Floor	Dia. of Entrance	Height above Ground (Ft.)
Bluebird	5 x 5	8	6	1½	5 to 10
Robin	6 x 8	8	2 adjacent sides open		6 to 15
Chickadee	4 x 4	8 to 10	8	1	6 to 15
Nuthatch	4 x 4	8 to 10	8	1¼	12 to 20
Wren	4 x 4	6 to 8	1 to 6	⅞	6 to 10
Tree Swallow	5 x 5	6	1 to 6	1½	10 to 15
Barn Swallow	6 x 6	6	2 adjacent sides open		8 to 12
Purple Martin	6 x 6	6	1	2½	15 to 20
Song Sparrow	6 x 6	6	3 sides open		2 to 4
House Finch	6 x 6	6	4	2	8 to 12
Phoebe	6 x 6	6	2 adjacent sides open		8 to 12
Woodpecker Downy	6 x 6	12 to 15	12	1½ to 2	12 to 20
Woodpecker	4 x 4	8 to 10	8	1¼	6 to 20
Flicker	7 x 7	16 to 18	16	2½	6 to 20
Screech Owl	8 x 8	12 to 15	12	3	10 to 30

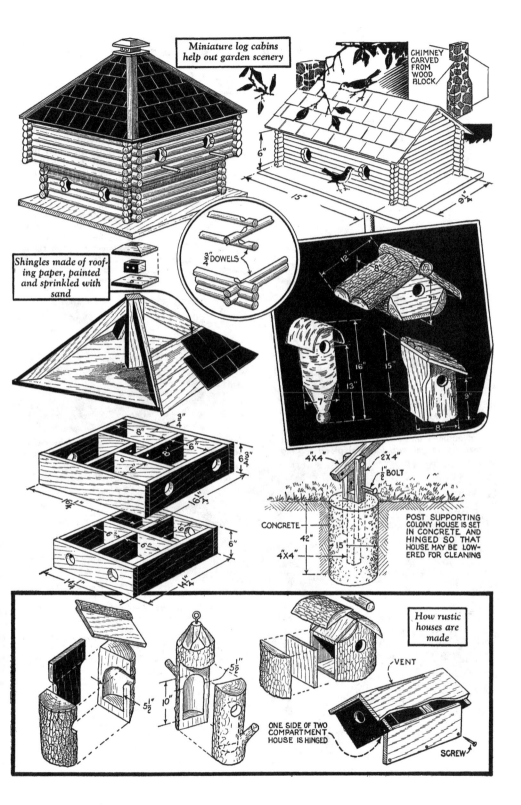

Miniature log cabins help out garden scenery

CHIMNEY CARVED FROM WOOD BLOCK

6"

15"

9½"

Shingles made of roofing paper, painted and sprinkled with sand

¾" DOWELS

12"

8"

7"

16"

15"

13"

7"

9"

8"

¾"

8"

8"

6"

6¾"

16½"

6"

6"

6"

6"

14½"

4½"

4"X4"

2"X4"

½" BOLT

CONCRETE

42"

15"

4"X4"

POST SUPPORTING COLONY HOUSE IS SET IN CONCRETE, AND HINGED SO THAT HOUSE MAY BE LOWERED FOR CLEANING

How rustic houses are made

VENT

5½"

1" 5½"

5½" 10"

ONE SIDE OF TWO COMPARTMENT HOUSE IS HINGED

SCREW

5

Boomerangs are

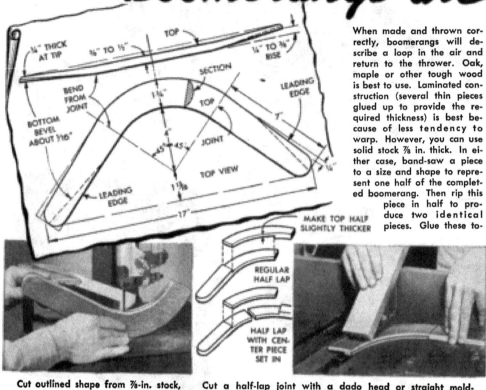

When made and thrown correctly, boomerangs will describe a loop in the air and return to the thrower. Oak, maple or other tough wood is best to use. Laminated construction (several thin pieces glued up to provide the required thickness) is best because of less tendency to warp. However, you can use solid stock ⅞ in. thick. In either case, band-saw a piece to a size and shape to represent one half of the completed boomerang. Then rip this piece in half to produce two identical pieces. Glue these to-

MAKE TOP HALF SLIGHTLY THICKER

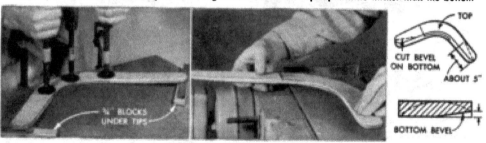

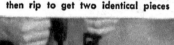

REGULAR HALF LAP

HALF LAP WITH CENTER PIECE SET IN

Cut outlined shape from ⅞-in. stock, then rip to get two identical pieces

Cut a half-lap joint with a dado head or straight molding cutter. Leave the top lap a little thicker than the bottom

¼" BLOCKS UNDER TIPS

TOP

CUT BEVEL ON BOTTOM

ABOUT 5"

BOTTOM BEVEL

Glue the joint. Spring the tips upward on blocks to get required rise

Sand or plane the bottom bevel—about 1/16 in. probably will be enough. You can increase it later if it is necessary

EDGES TOO BLUNT

AVOID THIS

SHARP EDGE — SMOOTH CURVE

CORRECT SHAPE

Plane the top surface from joint to tip

Round the top surface with a wood rasp and sand smooth

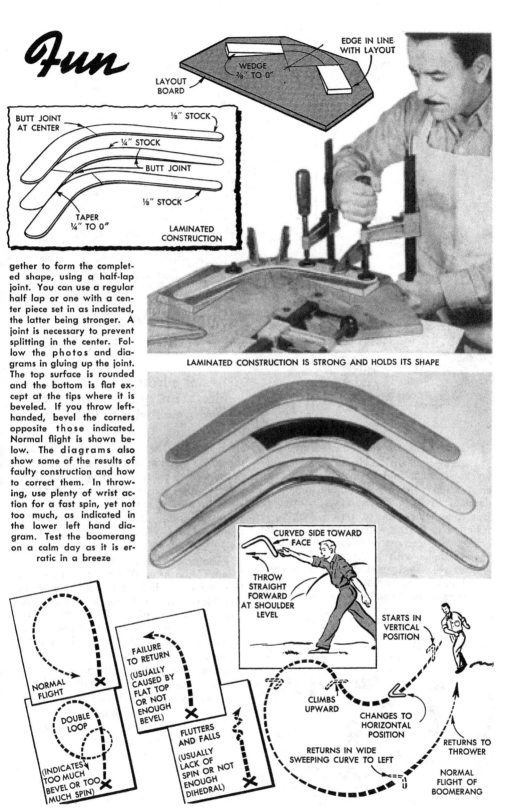

Fun

EDGE IN LINE WITH LAYOUT

LAYOUT BOARD

WEDGE ⅛" TO 0"

BUTT JOINT AT CENTER

⅛" STOCK

¼" STOCK

BUTT JOINT

⅛" STOCK

TAPER ¼" TO 0"

LAMINATED CONSTRUCTION

gether to form the completed shape, using a half-lap joint. You can use a regular half lap or one with a center piece set in as indicated, the latter being stronger. A joint is necessary to prevent splitting in the center. Follow the photos and diagrams in gluing up the joint. The top surface is rounded and the bottom is flat except at the tips where it is beveled. If you throw left-handed, bevel the corners opposite those indicated. Normal flight is shown below. The diagrams also show some of the results of faulty construction and how to correct them. In throwing, use plenty of wrist action for a fast spin, yet not too much, as indicated in the lower left hand diagram. Test the boomerang on a calm day as it is erratic in a breeze

LAMINATED CONSTRUCTION IS STRONG AND HOLDS ITS SHAPE

CURVED SIDE TOWARD FACE

THROW STRAIGHT FORWARD AT SHOULDER LEVEL

STARTS IN VERTICAL POSITION

CLIMBS UPWARD

CHANGES TO HORIZONTAL POSITION

RETURNS TO THROWER

RETURNS IN WIDE SWEEPING CURVE TO LEFT

NORMAL FLIGHT OF BOOMERANG

NORMAL FLIGHT

FAILURE TO RETURN
(USUALLY CAUSED BY FLAT TOP OR NOT ENOUGH BEVEL)

DOUBLE LOOP

(INDICATES TOO MUCH BEVEL OR TOO MUCH SPIN)

FLUTTERS AND FALLS
(USUALLY LACK OF SPIN OR NOT ENOUGH DIHEDRAL)

7

IT'S TIME for

Aerial photography, novel kites and quick-acting reels lend new thrills to kite flying

THINK of the fun you'll have taking pictures—real aerial views of the countryside from a high-flying box kite. It's easy when you rig the simple apparatus detailed in Figs. 1 and 2. A triangular frame, to which the camera is lashed, is fastened to the kite string just below the bridle. The camera is lashed in the bottom triangle with a thread holding the shutter release against the pull of a rubber band. Underneath the string is a safety-razor blade sliding in a slotted stick

as in Fig. 1. When you pull the trip cord, the razor blade severs the string attached to the rubber band, thus tripping the shutter. Another arrangement, shown at the right in Fig. 2, makes use of a glowing string, the latter attached to a thread holding the shutter release. The string can be 4 or 5 in. long. No separate sling is used, the camera being lashed directly to the frame of the kite. When you're ready for launching, you light the end of the string and blow out the flame as soon as the string starts to glow. Then send up the kite in a hurry. When the glowing string reaches the thread holding the shutter, you have your picture. The secret of taking good pictures in this way is the selection of a day when the wind is blowing steady so that you can maneuver the kite into the desired position.

Fig. 4 details the type and average size of the kite required for carrying a small camera aloft. Such a kite will lift a pound or less in a very light breeze. It's simply a triangular box kite with wings, the frame being made from ¼ by ¼-in.

KITE FLYING

Fig. 3 detail labels: 1" SQUARES · 15" · STRINGS 120° APART · ⅛ BALSA · GREEN · YELLOW · TISSUE PAPER · 30" · ½ BALSA CLEATS · ⅛ BAMBOO HOOP 10" DIA. · 6" · BUILT UP OF 1/32 SHEET BALSA

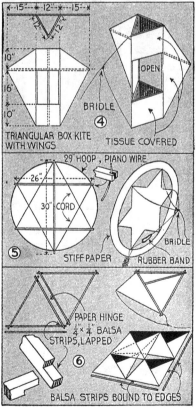

Fig. 4: 15" · 12" · 15" · 12" · 12" · 10" · 16" · 10" · BRIDLE · OPEN · TRIANGULAR BOX KITE WITH WINGS · TISSUE COVERED

Fig. 5: 26" · 30" CORD · STIFF PAPER · 29" HOOP, PIANO WIRE · BRIDLE · RUBBER BAND

Fig. 6: PAPER HINGE · ¼" × ¼" BALSA STRIPS, LAPPED · BALSA STRIPS BOUND TO EDGES

strips of either balsa or spruce and covered with medium heavy wrapping paper. In constructing this kite and others like those shown in Figs. 5 and 6, model-airplane cement is used to assemble the frame, and glue or wing dope will do to stick the paper to the frame.

Now for something different which you'll find in Fig. 3. Dragon kites demand accurate workmanship and some experimenting to get them into the air successfully. The disks should not only be extremely light, but accurately made and evenly balanced. Rings and balancing sticks are of bamboo about 1/16 in. in diameter, or lighter. Make the head of very thin strips of sheet balsa with cleats across the back as shown in the squared detail, Fig. 3. Streamers on the chin serve as a balance. A two-string bridle is attached to the top and bottom of the head. First, try out ten or twelve disks, then add others in decreasing diameters until the kite is the desired length.

A shark chasing a school of fish high above the housetops as in Fig. 8, will create a sensation. A box kite will keep several 10-ft. fish in the air in

9

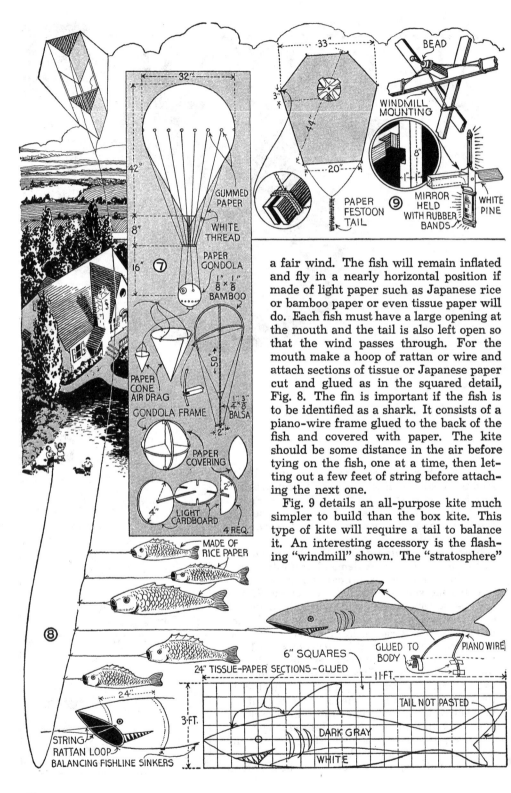

a fair wind. The fish will remain inflated and fly in a nearly horizontal position if made of light paper such as Japanese rice or bamboo paper or even tissue paper will do. Each fish must have a large opening at the mouth and the tail is also left open so that the wind passes through. For the mouth make a hoop of rattan or wire and attach sections of tissue or Japanese paper cut and glued as in the squared detail, Fig. 8. The fin is important if the fish is to be identified as a shark. It consists of a piano-wire frame glued to the back of the fish and covered with paper. The kite should be some distance in the air before tying on the fish, one at a time, then letting out a few feet of string before attaching the next one.

Fig. 9 details an all-purpose kite much simpler to build than the box kite. This type of kite will require a tail to balance it. An interesting accessory is the flashing "windmill" shown. The "stratosphere"

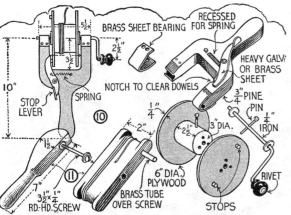

kite, Fig. 7, is designed for novelty, and must be made of light materials, slightly bowed at the back. With exception of the bow it is similar to the well-known two-stick kite with bowed top. A six-pointed star kite, Fig. 5, is not only easily made but is a striking design when the paper covering is of different color in bright shades. For example, use silver paper on the points, red for the center and blue for the circle. The star kite also requires a tail. Tetrahedral kites, Fig. 6, require a stronger wind for successful flying than do the flat or bowed kites. To make them, light balsa sticks are cut to lap and made into a pair of equilateral triangles. Match them up for size and then cover with paper. When dry, put a gummed paper strip or hinge along the edges of the triangle and with an extra stick, set them to form a "vee." Four of these can be built up to form a larger kite by binding a stick along the edges to keep the units together.

A simple hand reel is shown in Fig. 11. A piece of tubing over a screw makes a good crank. In Fig. 10 is a more elaborate job of the same general type, with a stop to prevent the string running out when the hand is off the crank. To wind the string evenly on the drum a cam-arm design is shown in Fig. 12. The cam is merely a wooden cylinder mounted eccentrically, and the arm made of plywood. The slower the cam revolves in relation to the drum, the better job of winding it will do. The two-crank model in Fig. 13 gives a variable winding speed. For fast winding the geared-up crank is used; the direct crank for slower and heavier work. One of the best arrangements for handling a large kite is the free-wheeling reel with a clutch, shown in Fig. 14. The crankshaft is divided in the middle—one end fixed in the hub by means of a pin, the other sliding in and out. Normally it is forced in by a coil spring, bringing into contact the two clutch faces of garnet paper cemented to rubber.

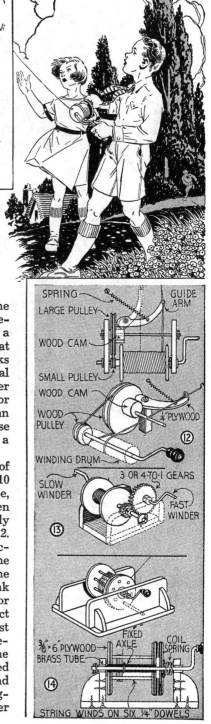

This Super Bean Shooter Has a Magazine

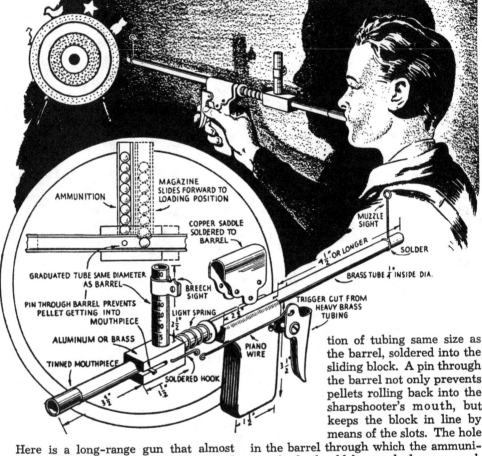

MAGAZINE SLIDES FORWARD TO LOADING POSITION

AMMUNITION

COPPER SADDLE SOLDERED TO BARREL

MUZZLE SIGHT

1½" OR LONGER

SOLDER

GRADUATED TUBE SAME DIAMETER AS BARREL

BREECH SIGHT

BRASS TUBE ¼" INSIDE DIA.

PIN THROUGH BARREL PREVENTS PELLET GETTING INTO MOUTHPIECE

LIGHT SPRING

TRIGGER CUT FROM HEAVY BRASS TUBING

ALUMINUM OR BRASS

PIANO WIRE

TINNED MOUTHPIECE

SOLDERED HOOK

Here is a long-range gun that almost gets into the naval class of artillery, and shoots a surprising distance with great accuracy. Although it falls in the classification of a bean shooter, it is designed to use pearl tapioca pellets for ammunition and is quite harmless, since these are neither as hard nor as heavy as beans. They are ideal for the purpose because they are round and slide easily through the ¼-in. barrel, which may be 24 in. long. The mouthpiece of the barrel should be tinned with solder because of the unpleasant taste of the brass tube. Mount the barrel on a wood hand grip as shown, after the magazine has been fitted. The latter consists of either a brass or an aluminum block drilled to fit over the tube so that it slides easily but without any play. The magazine is merely another sec-

tion of tubing same size as the barrel, soldered into the sliding block. A pin through the barrel not only prevents pellets rolling back into the sharpshooter's mouth, but keeps the block in line by means of the slots. The hole in the barrel through which the ammunition feeds should be amply large enough to prevent jamming. Graduations for the rear sight must be marked by trial.

Spring Improves Stove-Lid Lifter

RIVETS

SPRING

To prevent a stove lid from falling off of a lifter, rivet a flat spring to it as shown. The free end of the spring should be bent upward so that it will slip over the surface of the lid easily. The spring grips the lid and helps hold it, but not so tight that the lifter is hard to remove.

Aerial CLUBHOUSE

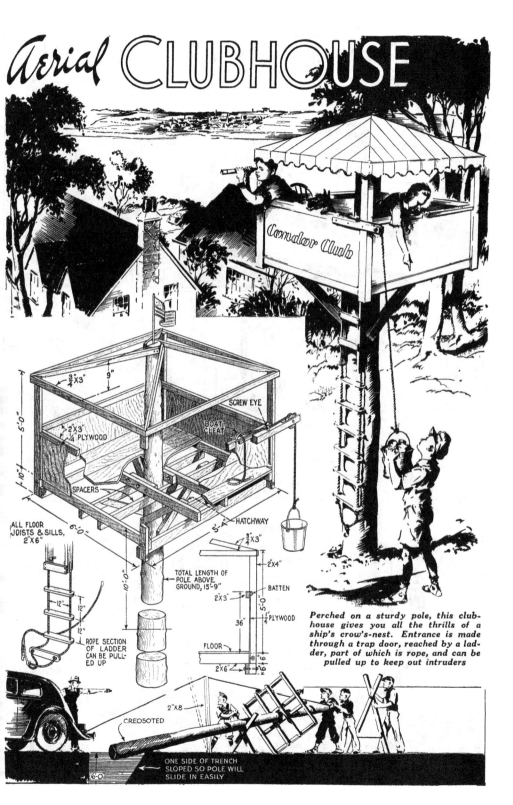

Condor Club

ALL FLOOR JOISTS & SILLS, 2"X6"

¾"X3"   9"

2"X3"
¾ PLYWOOD

SPACERS

SCREW EYE

BOAT CLEAT

6'-0"

5'-0"

4'-0"

HATCHWAY

5'-A"

¾"X3"

2"X4"

2"X3"

BATTEN

36"

½ PLYWOOD

5'-0"

FLOOR

2"X6"

6'-9"

6'-9"

TOTAL LENGTH OF POLE ABOVE GROUND, 15'-9"

10'-0"

12"   12"

12"   12"

ROPE SECTION OF LADDER CAN BE PULL-ED UP

2"X8"

CREOSOTED

6'-0"

ONE SIDE OF TRENCH SLOPED SO POLE WILL SLIDE IN EASILY

Perched on a sturdy pole, this clubhouse gives you all the thrills of a ship's crow's-nest. Entrance is made through a trap door, reached by a ladder, part of which is rope, and can be pulled up to keep out intruders

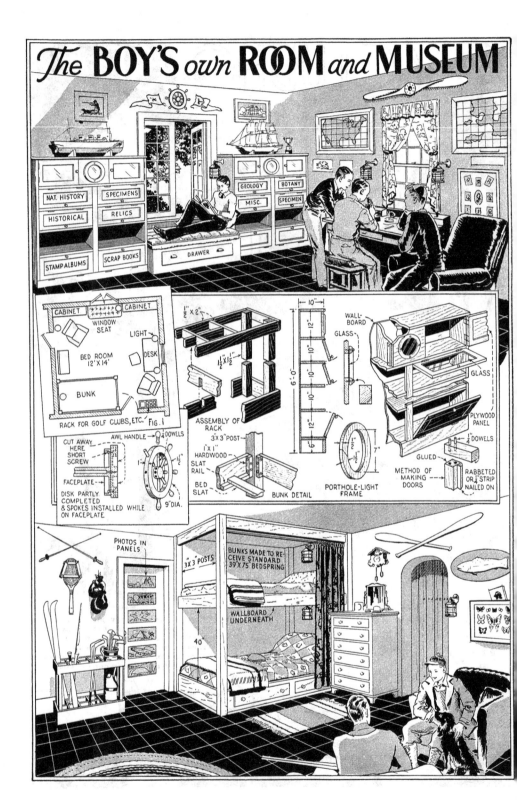

The BOY'S own ROOM and MUSEUM

Mail-Pouch Catcher Gives Realistic Action

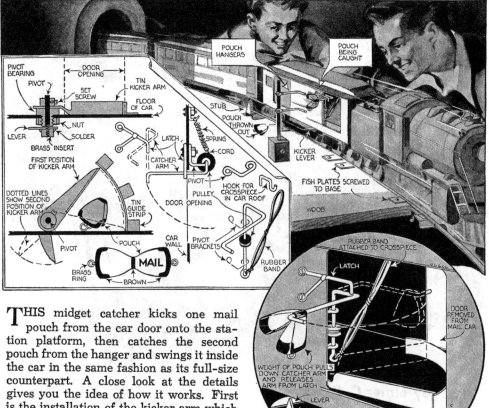

THIS midget catcher kicks one mail pouch from the car door onto the station platform, then catches the second pouch from the hanger and swings it inside the car in the same fashion as its full-size counterpart. A close look at the details gives you the idea of how it works. First is the installation of the kicker arm which throws the pouch out the car door. This is a tin angle swinging on a pivot installed just inside the door in the manner shown. A curved guide strip is soldered to the floor of the car to hold the pouch in the proper position. A stub or lug soldered to the track engages a lever attached to the kicker pivot to actuate the arm. No dimensions are given on these parts because you have to make them to fit the car in hand. The catcher is really a separate unit supported on two pivot brackets of bent wire attached to the side of the car. The arm and latch are also bent from wire to the shape indicated. A tiny sheave, made from two sheet-metal disks and a small housing, is soldered to the arm. One end of a light cord wound around the sheave several turns is attached to a return spring as you see it in the details. Now, when you have the arrangement assembled as shown in the circle above, make sure that it works freely without binding at any point.

The mail pouch is loaded with small lead shot and when caught by the arm its weight is sufficient to pull the arm down slightly, releasing it from the latch. Then the coil spring, attached to the sheave and the car wall, pulls the arm inside the door as indicated by the dotted lines. When the pouch is removed and the arm swung back to position, the tension of the rubber band shown holds the arm under the latch. Some experiment will be necessary to get the hanger located in the proper position on the platform. Of course, the latter must be attached to the track so that it does not shift and throw the hanger out of line.

⊄Stair carpet will last longer and wear more evenly if you purchase it half a yard too long, and fold it in at the top and bottom of the stairs; as the carpet wears on the edges of the treads, move it a trifle.

Model Railway TRACK LAYOUT takes small space

By Elmer C. Black

DESIGNED for operating one or two trains on a moderate sized platform, this complete layout, Fig. 1, has a main line, branch line, and a siding, which is also used to reverse the direction of the trains, those on each line being independently controlled. Also, the layout provides a "scenic route," permitting a train to cover the entire track system by operating but one switch.

Use a base of nonwarping material, such as hard-pressed board, and lay the track as in Fig. 2, cutting short lengths of straight track to fit at the points marked "X." Place insulating pins in the center rails where indicated to separate the circuits, and wire the layout as shown. Insulating pins in the outside rails of the nonderailing type switches should be placed according to the manufacturer's instructions. On the underside of the

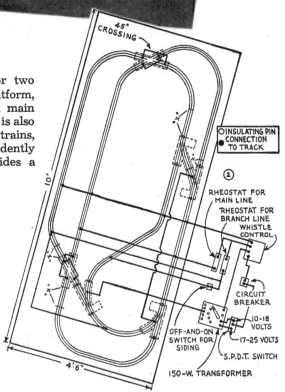

45° CROSSING

○ INSULATING PIN
● CONNECTION TO TRACK

RHEOSTAT FOR MAIN LINE

RHEOSTAT FOR BRANCH LINE

WHISTLE CONTROL

CIRCUIT BREAKER

10-18 VOLTS

OFF-AND-ON SWITCH FOR SIDING

17-25 VOLTS

S.P.D.T. SWITCH

150-W. TRANSFORMER

10'

4'6"

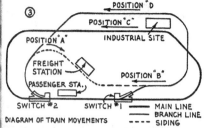

POSITION "D"
POSITION "C"
POSITION "A"
INDUSTRIAL SITE
FREIGHT STATION
POSITION "B"
PASSENGER STA.
SWITCH #2   SWITCH #1 —— MAIN LINE
—— BRANCH LINE
DIAGRAM OF TRAIN MOVEMENTS   ---- SIDING

crossings, a piece of tire tape is placed between the two metal connector strips to separate the circuits at these points. After wiring, if the proper current does not reach the track, reverse the two wires leading from the whistle controller. Remote-control equipment with nonderailing switches will prove most satisfactory, and the operating controls are brought to a central panel for efficient control of the trains.

A s.p.d.t. toggle switch steps up the voltage when running two trains at once, and an off-and-on toggle switch in the circuit to the siding controls trains on this section. Separate rheostats regulate the train speeds on either line. If desired, lead weights may be placed in a car of the faster train to balance the speeds to keep the trains the same distance apart on the short section between switch No. 2 and switch No. 1, Fig. 3, where both trains use the same track. Use at least a 150-watt transformer for the power source. To protect the whistle controller, do not blow the whistle when both trains are running.

Many interesting train movements can be executed on this layout. For a "scenic route," start a train from position "A," Fig. 3, running it in the direction of the arrow.

With switch No. 1 closed, the train will circle around the entire layout without attention. To reverse direction of a train, open switch No. 1 and run train from position "B" over siding and back to the original position. For continuous running of two trains at one time, bring a train to position "C" and "D" respectively. Start the train at position "D" on the branch line, and when it passes the crossing start train at "C." By alternately opening and closing switch No. 1, each train can be kept to its own line or shifted to the other as desired. Use the rheostats on each line to control train speeds to avoid smash-ups at the crossings. Suggested locations for a freight and passenger station and an industrial site are indicated in the diagram.

Auto-Wheel Rim in Wire Fence Makes Safe Gate for Dog

After his dog had become injured from jumping through a barb-wire fence, one farmer provided a gate through which a dog could pass in safety. The gate was made by wedging an auto-wheel rim between the fence wires as indicated.

TIRE RIM

Long Tongs to Right Derailed Model-Train Cars

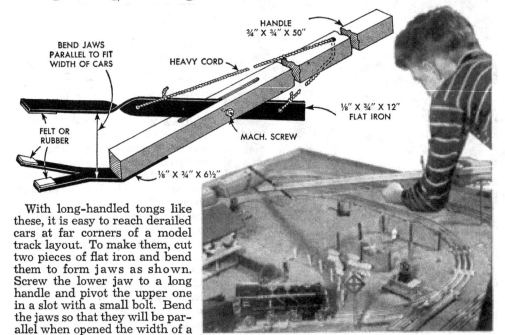

BEND JAWS PARALLEL TO FIT WIDTH OF CARS

HANDLE ¾" X ¾" X 50"

HEAVY CORD

⅛" X ¾" X 12" FLAT IRON

FELT OR RUBBER

MACH. SCREW

⅛" X ¾" X 6½"

With long-handled tongs like these, it is easy to reach derailed cars at far corners of a model track layout. To make them, cut two pieces of flat iron and bend them to form jaws as shown. Screw the lower jaw to a long handle and pivot the upper one in a slot with a small bolt. Bend the jaws so that they will be parallel when opened the width of a car, and run a cord from a hole in the one end of the movable jaw up through a hole near the end of the handle and back to a hole in the opposite end of the jaw. To use the tongs, you simply pull on the upper cord to open the jaw, slide it under the derailed car and then pull on the lower cord to grip the car.

—C. Elmer Black, Philadelphia, Pa.

Guide Wire on Ruler to Make Straight Lines With Brush

An ordinary ruler may be used as a straightedge for drawing lines with a small brush if it is fitted with a taut wire as indicated to keep the brush away from the edge of the ruler. As indicated, wire nails are inserted through holes near the ruler ends and are clinched into grooves on the underside of the ruler where they are secured with small staples. The head ends of the nails then are bent over at right angles toward the ruler edge and notched with a file. The wire is pulled taut, wound into the grooves and soldered to secure it.

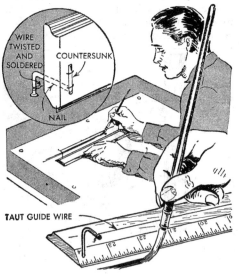

WIRE TWISTED AND SOLDERED

COUNTERSUNK

NAIL

TAUT GUIDE WIRE

Tweezers Made From Toothpicks Handle Delicate Work

Modelmakers and others who work with tiny wood pieces can improvise a pair of tweezers for this work by gluing three toothpicks together as indicated. The tweezers may be used as gluing clamps to hold pieces together while the glue dries, or to grip and hold small screws, bolts or nuts while inserting them.

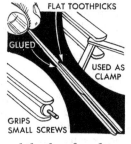

FLAT TOOTHPICKS

GLUED

USED AS CLAMP

GRIPS SMALL SCREWS

Electric Train Switches Closed Automatically

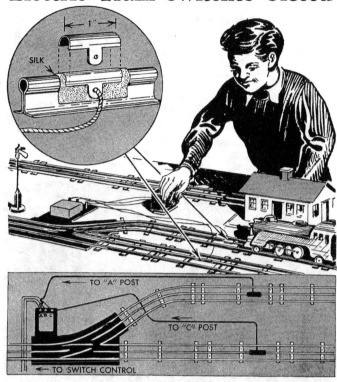

SILK

Whether manually or electrically operated, switches for toy electric trains require an operator's attention to be sure that they are always in correct position to receive an approaching train. However, in the case of electrically operated switches, this constant vigilance can be avoided by fitting the track with metal clips and connecting them to the switch-operating mechanism as shown. When an engine passes over one of the clips, momentary contact is made to close the switch automatically. The clips are thin brass, tin or copper strips, bent to fit over the center rail from which they are insulated by pieces of silk. The clips should be located a train's length from the switch so proper contact is made in plenty of time.

TO "A" POST

A B C

TO "C" POST

← TO SWITCH CONTROL

Mousetrap Supplies "Firepower" for Simple Toy Cannon

In assembling this toy cannon, which uses shells cut from wooden dowels, you won't have to worry about fitting a trigger and spring mechanism, as firepower is provided by an ordinary mousetrap. After screwing the trap to a solid wood base, a suitable barrel is turned, bored and mounted so that the trap jaw strikes the center of it when sprung. Loading is accomplished quickly by setting the trap and inserting a shell, leaving the end of it project slightly as shown. Then the trigger is pressed to spring the trap and "fire" the cannon.

—Thomas M. Stradley, Jeffersonville, Ind.

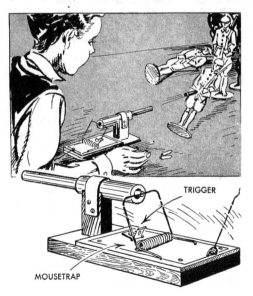

TRIGGER

MOUSETRAP

Model-Airplane Motor Cylinders Imitated With Capsules

Instead of tediously carving imitation cylinders from wood to simulate the motor of a model airplane, one hobbyist uses empty medicine capsules. Obtainable in various sizes, the capsules are merely glued around the shaped nose of the plane as indicated. Spaced wrappings of fine thread around the capsules give the appearance of cooling fins.

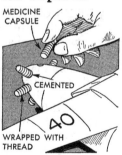

MEDICINE CAPSULE

CEMENTED

WRAPPED WITH THREAD

Model GAS-DRIVEN

by JOE OTT

Here's an exact scale model of a famous racing monoplane, "Mister Mulligan," one-time winner of the Bendix Trophy and the Thompson Trophy at the National Air Races. The model is scaled down to a wingspread of 66 in., and is driven by a tiny single-cylinder gasoline motor swinging a 15-in. propeller at 3,000 r.p.m. Under good flying conditions the model will attain a speed of approximately 18 m.p.h. The total weight of the model ship ready to fly is 3½ lbs., or 56 ounces

Fuselage Framework and Landing Gear

ALTHOUGH it was a great thrill to fly your first rubber-band model plane, it's nothing compared to the realism of flying a gas-driven model! Midget gasoline motors that develop from ⅛ to ⅓ hp. will fly readily a 5 to 8-ft. plane weighing up to 5 lbs. The average cost of the motor is about $15.00 and all the materials needed to build the model of "Mister Mulligan" cost around $3.00.

Before proceeding with any of the details, it's a good idea to become familiar with the entire general construction of the model. When the actual construction is

started, go thoroughly and completely in detail over the particular unit being assembled. Then lay out in single lines a full-size drawing of the fuselage, landing gear and tail wheel as in Fig. 1.

Fuselage: Looking at Figs. 2, 3, 4, and 8, begin with the center line which is the bottom longeron and which is the main longitudinal member in the body. One body height is given in the cross sections at station 5. This height continues through stations 6 and 7. From here through to station 12 there is a gradual taper above the center line. The top longeron tapers

PLANE ··

is speedy flyer

downward until it meets the given height of station 12. The distances between stations are given in the side view, Fig. 8. After the side view has been drawn, the construction can be started and the parts are placed directly over the drawn lines as in Fig. 7. Note that the heights for sections from stations 8 to 11 incl., are not given but must be checked on the full-size layout. The top and bottom longerons are placed in position, working directly over the center of the lines. Pin the longerons in place. When the uprights are fitted between the longerons they will tend to force the longerons against the pins, firmly holding them in position. Two sides exactly alike are constructed, one directly over the other, and separated with wax paper. This done, you make a full-sized layout of the top of the fuselage. Check the top dimensions at stations 5, 7 and 12. Draw the lines tangent to these dimensions, permitting the rest to fall in line. After the two sides are dry, place them right side up and pin in a similar manner to the board as specified for the side view. The cross braces are cut and fitted first at the points dimensioned and then at those not marked. After the top and bottom cross braces have been cemented in, the main part of the fuselage is complete. When constructing a part be sure to refer to the parts list so that the proper materials are used. The body so far should have been constructed entirely from bass wood or sugar pine. Sand all pieces before cutting to exact length. Balsa wood can be used throughout for the construction, but for the additional few ounces of weight, pine or bass wood gives greater strength and resiliency. From the bottom longeron to the extreme bottom of the fuselage the construction will be 1/16-in. sheet balsa and 1/8-in. balsa bracing, with a center piece of pine or bass running the full length from station 4 to 12. Note that a triangular section is built up underneath each station and small semi-circular pieces are added to complete the circular shape of the underside. At points not dimensioned, check the distance across the lower cross brace, then draw a circle equaling this diameter

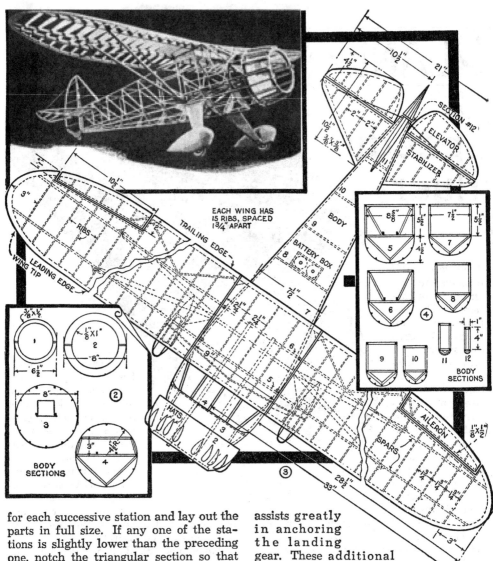

EACH WING HAS
15 RIBS, SPACED
1¾" APART

BODY

BATTERY BOX

RIBS

TRAILING EDGE

LEADING EDGE

WING TIP

SECTION #12
ELEVATOR
STABILIZER

BODY SECTIONS

AILERON

SPARS

HATS

BODY
SECTIONS

for each successive station and lay out the parts in full size. If any one of the stations is slightly lower than the preceding one, notch the triangular section so that the longeron forms a straight line for the greater part of the distance between stations 6 and 12 and a slight gradual curve between stations 4 and 6. The motor supports, which are ¼ by ½-in. pine, should be fitted in on top of the bottom cross braces between the two lower longerons. The distance between these supports will depend entirely upon the motor selected. After the motor mounts have been placed, check the views of the model and note that the triangular braces from the top station 5 to the motor brace are added on each side. An additional triangular brace is placed between stations 4 and 5, which

assists greatly in anchoring the landing gear. These additional braces may be made of balsa. A similar triangular brace is also placed on each side of the fuselage from the top down at station 6. This brace helps to eliminate side sway when the wings are in place. Additional bracing can be added by cementing small gussets in the corners on the main longerons at stations 4 to 7 inclusive. A gusset is a small flat triangular piece of balsa usually joining an upright, a cross brace and a longeron.

Motor Cowl: The small wooden streamlined sections cemented on top of the motor-cowl covering are hats and on the

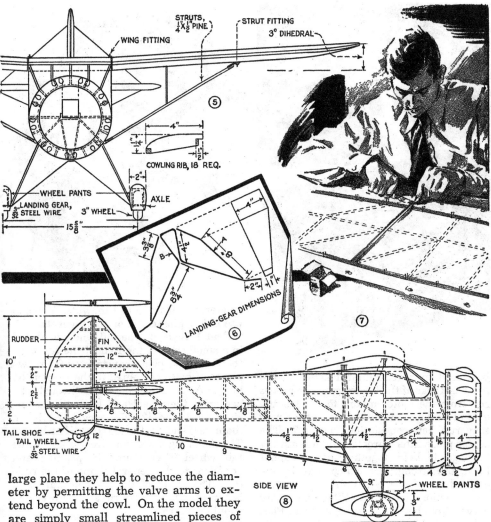

WING FITTING

STRUTS, $\frac{1}{4} \times \frac{1}{2}$ PINE

STRUT FITTING

3° DIHEDRAL

⑤

4"

COWLING RIB, 18 REQ.

2"

WHEEL PANTS

AXLE

LANDING GEAR, $\frac{3}{32}$ STEEL WIRE

3" WHEEL

$15\frac{5}{8}$"

LANDING-GEAR DIMENSIONS

⑥

⑦

RUDDER

FIN

10"

12"

2"

7"

$2\frac{1}{2}$

2

$4\frac{7}{8}$ $4\frac{7}{8}$ $4\frac{7}{8}$ $4\frac{7}{8}$

$4\frac{1}{8}$ $4\frac{1}{2}$ $4\frac{1}{2}$ $5\frac{1}{4}$ $1\frac{1}{16}$ 4"

TAIL SHOE

TAIL WHEEL

$\frac{1}{32}$ STEEL WIRE

12 11 10 9 8 7 6 5 4 3 2 1

SIDE VIEW

⑧

9"

3"

WHEEL PANTS

large plane they help to reduce the diameter by permitting the valve arms to extend beyond the cowl. On the model they are simply small streamlined pieces of balsa sanded to shape. There are 18 of these, equally spaced in pairs.

Stations 1 and 2 give the diameters and the cross-sectional sizes of the rings required for the motor cowl. Note in Figs. 9 and 10 that the front part of the body at stations 2 and 3 has a wall completely constructed of balsa wood. There is a small opening leading directly from station 3 to station 4 under the front of the windshield as in Fig. 2. This is a hot-air vent and is covered with balsa on all sides except the top. When the motor is entirely enclosed the hot air escapes through this vent. The motor cowl is constructed of two rings which are sawed from large flat sections of balsa, cemented together and assembled with 18 cowling ribs. The cowling is as-

sembled in two halves. The lower half is firmly cemented in position and is a part of the body. The top half is loose and is held in place by rubber bands and removes in a jiffy, permitting complete examination and checking of the motor, the gas tank and the spark coil.

Landing Gear: The landing gear, Figs. 5 and 6, is constructed of $\frac{3}{32}$-in. steel wire. The unit visible in the side view, Fig. 8, is made in one piece, but note that you must have a right and left unit. The center section is also made in one piece and continues through the wheel pants. The landing-gear frame is filled with $\frac{1}{8}$-in. balsa sheeting and is attached to the motor mounts between stations 5 and 6, where it

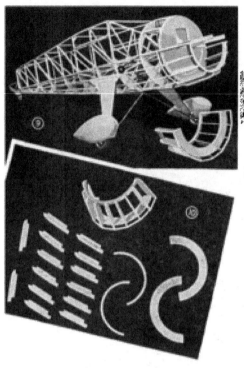

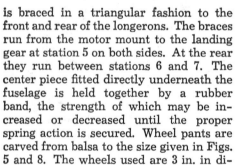

ameter, and from ½ to 1 in. wide. You can use either pneumatic or solid wheels.

Rear Fuselage: The tail wheel is placed in a small shoe at the rear of the fuselage, the mounting being constructed from two pieces of balsa cemented to the rear of the body. A 1/32-in. wire passes through the center of the wheel and back to the upright at station 12. The wheel is 1 in. in diameter and is turned from hardwood. The small rigid section directly above the tail wheel is cemented in position and conforms to the general shape of the rudder. The width of the body at station 12 is 1 in., and the rudder rib at the lower end should conform.

is braced in a triangular fashion to the front and rear of the longerons. The braces run from the motor mount to the landing gear at station 5 on both sides. At the rear they run between stations 6 and 7. The center piece fitted directly underneath the fuselage is held together by a rubber band, the strength of which may be increased or decreased until the proper spring action is secured. Wheel pants are carved from balsa to the size given in Figs. 5 and 8. The wheels used are 3 in. in di-

MATERIAL LIST

FUSELAGE	DIMENSIONS	NO. PIECES
Longerons, cross braces and uprights	5/32 x 5/32 x 42 in.	12 pine or basswood
Cross braces	5/32 x 5/32 x 42 in.	12 balsa
Motor supports	¼ x ½ x 18 in.	2 pine or basswood
Body formers	1/16 x 2 x 24 in.	6 balsa
Stringers	⅛ x ⅛ x 42 in.	12 balsa
MOTOR COWL		
Circular ring—front cut to shape	⅜ x ½ in.	1 set balsa
Circular ring—rear cut to shape	⅛ x 1 in.	1 set basla
Cowling ribs	1/16-in. sheet 3 x 24 in.	1 balsa
LANDING GEAR		
Bracing and axle	10 ft. of 3/32-in. piano wire	1 steel
Wheels	½ x 3 in. diameter	2 hardwood
Tail wheel	3/16 x 1in. diameter	1 hardwood
Wheel pants (cores)	¾ x 4 x 10 in.	2 balsa
Wheel pants (covers)	⅛ x 3 x 7 in.	4 balsa
Landing-gear struts	⅛ x 4 x 7 in.	2 balsa

Gas-Driven

PART II

MODEL PLANE

Rudder—Wings—Covering
Motor Installation

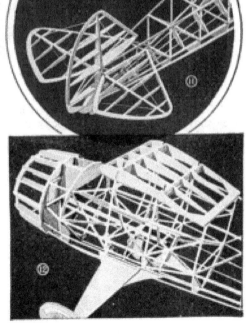

TAKING up the fin and rudder next, you sketch a full-size layout of the parts in Fig. 11, leaving a ⅛-in. space between the rudder and the bottom part of the tapered fuselage section. To do this, you can refer back to the plan view in Part I. Vertical members of the rudder and fin are tapered from the 1-in. width at the bottom to ³⁄₁₆ in. at the top. The leading and trailing edges are assembled first. Then the ribs are put in one at a time and fitted, starting at the bottom and working toward the top, small pins being used to hold the ribs in place until the cement sets. To keep the rudder square, a cross brace is placed from the upright of the second rib to the bottom rib near the trailing edge. After assembling, the parts are sanded to their proper streamlined shape. The rudder and fin are hinged at three points equally spaced with small strips of tin, ¹⁄₆₄ in. thick and ¼ in. wide. These pieces are forced

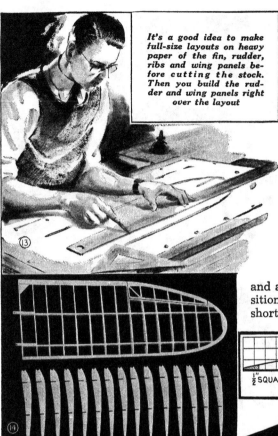

It's a good idea to make full-size layouts on heavy paper of the fin, rudder, ribs and wing panels before cutting the stock. Then you build the rudder and wing panels right over the layout

RIB SECTION, ⅟₆" SHEET BALSA

½" SQUARES

RIBS ARE CUT FROM SHAPED BLOCK ON THE CIRCULAR SAW

in. The center section, upon completion, is cemented in position against the top longeron on which a cross brace ½ in. high has been cemented to give the wing the correct angle of incidence.

Construction of the wing is similar to the center section and should be assembled over a full-size layout made from the plan view in Part I. Thirteen ribs are used in each panel, Figs. 14 and 16, and are spaced equally with the exception of the last one. The wing tips are cut from flat sheets and assembled in three sections. The front part is cut from ⅜-in. stock and the two rear parts from ³⁄₁₆-in. stock. The two ribs near the wing tips are less in height and are tapered to fit when placed in position. Also, the last five ribs are a trifle shorter. When constructing the wing pan-

through the uprights, bent over on the inside and cemented. They are flexible enough to permit bending the rudder either way. The hinge construction of the stabilizer and elevators is the same. The fin, rudder, stabilizers and elevators are covered before they are attached to the body permanently with cement.

Wings and Center Section: A full-size layout of the wing rib should be sketched as in Fig. 13, and this pattern cemented to a block of balsa wood which in turn is sawed to shape, Fig. 15, including the notches for the leading edge, the spars and a part of the trailing edge. A block, 3½ to 5 in. high, will be sufficient. After the outline has been formed, the ribs are sliced off as in Fig. 17. Allow ten extra ribs to cover possible breakage. The center section, Fig. 12, should be constructed first, the end ribs being double thickness, or ⅛ els, be sure to make a left and a right-hand unit. Now, when the parts have all dried, you cut out a section for the aileron, adding a few extra parts to complete this unit. These consist of two additional end ribs and a spar for the front part of the aileron, also a small spar cemented to the wing. The ailerons are attached at three points with small bands of tin, 1/64 by 1/4 in.

Wing Struts: The wing struts are made of pine. A 3° dihedral at the wing tips equals about 2-in. inclination for each tip. Although the length of the struts is given, it is advisable to cut and fit the parts with the model partly set up. The metal pieces that hold the wings to the center section are cut from

After covering fuselage and wings, the parts are sprayed with water, allowed to dry thoroughly, then given two coats of airplane wing dope. When dry this is followed with a coat of white lacquer applied with a camel's-hair brush

1/32-in. sheet metal, 1/4 in. wide and 1 1/2 in. long. Bolts are attached to the center section and are both cemented and tied, the threaded ends projecting upward 1/2 in. Two bolts in each wing project on the underside 1/2 in. below the wood parts. Triangular blocks of balsa forced against the spar and the rib hold them in place securely. Lugs for strut bolts on the body are attached first to a piece of balsa running across the inside of the fuselage at station 6. This piece is fitted in advance, the bolts attached with lugs which are wrapped with thread and cemented as in Fig. 21. The whole arrangement allows the wings to be detached from the fuse-

lage when the model is being transported.

Mounting the Motor: Now, before continuing, it's best to mount the motor and test it. With the motor in place, the tiny gasoline tank and spark coil are mounted on the body bulkhead as in Fig. 23. Because of the probability of breaking wire connections, make small pig tails leading from the spark plug to the high-tension side of the coil. As three volts are required for operation, two small 1 1/2-volt flashlight cells are soldered together in series with long wire leads soldered on. The leads go through the body and to the outside between stations 4 and 5 where a midget radio jack is used to break the circuit. The dry cells are located to the rear of station 8 in a balsa-wood box, made sufficiently large to permit wedging the batteries firmly in place. A trap door allows entry to the battery box as in Fig. 20. Positive and negative leads should be marked on the fuselage for connecting

27

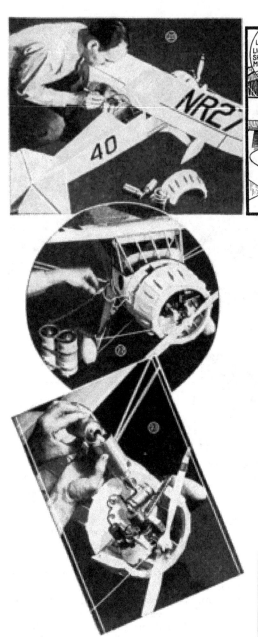

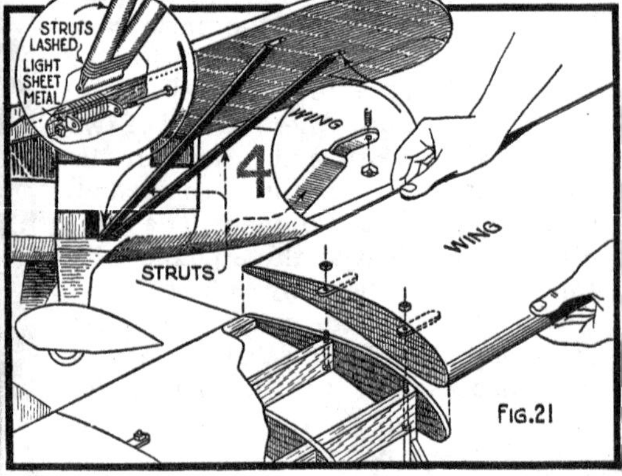

FIG.21

it reaches through to the outside of the motor cowl. The motor should be thoroughly checked, using both the external dry cells and the small ones. All of these small motors are of the two-cycle variety.

Material List

STABILIZER AND RUDDER

4 Spars, balsa, ⅛ x ¾ x 24 in.
4 Ribs, balsa, 1/16 x 2 x 24 in.
2 Leading Edge Spars, balsa, ⅜ x ⅜ x 24 in.
2 Trailing Edge Cut to Curve, balsa, 3/16 x ⅜ in.

WING MATERIAL

3 Leading Edge Spars, balsa, ⅜ x ⅜ x 24 in.
3 Front Spar, balsa, ⅛ x ¾ x 24 in.
3 Rear Spar, balsa, ⅛ x ½ x 24 in.
3 Trailing Edge, balsa, 3/16 x ⅝ x 24 in.
2 Wing Tips, Front, balsa, ⅜ x ⅜ in., cut to curve
2 Wing Tips, Rear, balsa, 3/16 x ⅝ in., cut to curve
30 Ribs, balsa, 1/16 x 1½ x 11 in.
10 Sets Bolts and Nuts, iron, 1 x 2/56 in.
10 Lugs, iron, 1/32 x ¼ x ¾ in.
4 Struts, pine or basswood, ¼ x ½ x 24 in.

MISCELLANEOUS

1 Windshield, heavy celluloid, 12 x 12 in.
1 Battery Box, balsa, 1/16 x 3 x 12 in.
½ pt. White Lacquer
½ pt. Quick-Drying Model Airplane Cement
½ pt. Dope
12 Sheets heavy bamboo fiber paper, 15 x 20 in. Black Tissue for numbers and control outlines, cut to size
1 Motor and 15 in. Propeller, small bore, less than 1 in.
1 Ignition Coil, 3 volt, 3 oz.
½ oz. 400-volt Condenser

large dry cells, which are used for starting. The dry cells are connected to the leads with clips and the circuit to the small flashlight cells is so arranged that after the motor has been started, the small cells are cut in the circuit. Then the clips to the large cells are removed and the motor will continue to run. The exhaust pipe is lengthened with thin sheet metal so that

Covering: Heavy bamboo-fiber paper is used for covering. Between five and ten sheets are required, the number depending on the size of the sheets. The paper is fastened in place as in Fig. 18, with model airplane cement. All the separate units are covered and sprayed with water, allowed to dry and then given two light coats of standard airplane "dope," followed with a coat of white lacquer as in Fig. 19. Hand-holes are arranged on each side of the hot-air vent behind the motor cowling on the top side of the fuselage or directly in front of the celluloid windshield. This is the best place to hold the model while starting. The rudder and stabilizers are braced with heavy thread. Decorations such as No. "40" placed on the fuselage sides and "NR-273Y" placed one under-neath the left wing and another on top of the right wing as in Fig. 19, help to com-plete the job. Black tissue paper, ⅛ in. wide, is used to outline the controls. This is also carried around the windows and windshield and a ⅟₆₄-in. strip is cemented around the body at stations 4, 5 and 7.

Preparing the Model for Flight: After checking all the parts and having the mo-tor in running condition, a suitable field is selected for the first trial flights. The weather should be perfectly calm, early morning or late evening being the best time. Fill the tank with ½ oz. of gasoline as in Fig. 23, attach the external dry cells, crank the motor, and select a hard run-way. It is advisable to have an assistant on hand so that when the model is started, the two persons can follow along with the model near the wing tips to see that it is in perfect balance before allowing it to continue on its first flight. Gas models are not as a rule launched by hand. They are permitted to run along a runway just as the large ships. If the balance does not appear to be correct, adjustments can be made before the model gets out of hand.

Fish Line Waxed Easily

When your fish line needs waxing, get a small tin can and punch holes in the opposite sides for corks. Melt enough wax to come up over the corks and then thread the line on a darning needle and push it through the corks. Pulling the line through the melted wax slowly will impregnate every fiber.

Rubber Wheels for Model Plane from Ink Erasers

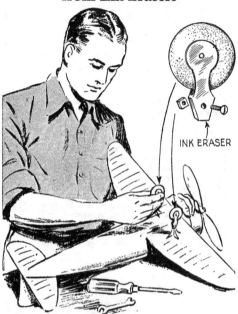

When the size of a model plane permits, use of ink erasers for wheels saves work

In some cases, round ink erasers provide good landing wheels for model planes. Simply remove the brush from the top of the eraser handle and attach the handle to the undercarriage of the plane with a small machine screw.

Turning Model Crankshafts

Here's a method of making a crankshaft for a model that will enable you to finish it right in the lathe without it springing or whipping badly. First, rough turn it to shape and finish the crank webs and the connect-ing-rod journal. Then solder a small brass block between the webs as shown. This stiffens the webs and journal so that the crank can be completed easily. When the crankshaft has been finished, heat it to melt the solder and then knock out the brass block, cleaning up the webs with a brush while the solder is still molten.

"Airplane" KITE
tests air currents at model meets

Knowledge of the velocity and action of the wind, which can often be obtained by using this kite, has saved many a model airplane from destruction. The kite is extremely sensitive and will record every puff by a jerk on the string. Made of 1/16 by 3/16-in. bamboo strips, the various parts are assembled by lapping the joints, which are cemented and lashed together with thread. A simple method of making a joint is to cut away a portion of the end of the frame member, leaving a thin strip which can be bent over, cemented and lashed to the adjoining member. Lengths of cord from the tail skid and the axle permit considerable latitude in adjusting the main string

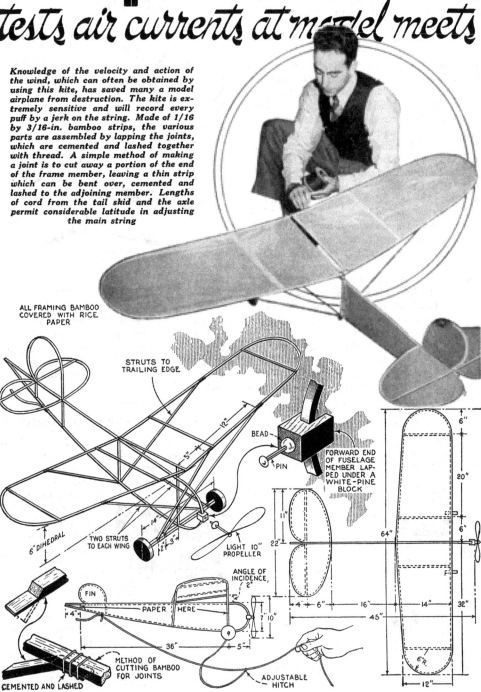

ALL FRAMING BAMBOO COVERED WITH RICE PAPER

STRUTS TO TRAILING EDGE

12"

5"

BEAD

PIN

FORWARD END OF FUSELAGE MEMBER LAPPED UNDER A WHITE-PINE BLOCK

6"

20"

6"

6" DIHEDRAL

TWO STRUTS TO EACH WING

14"

2" 3"

LIGHT 10" PROPELLER

11"

22"

64"

ANGLE OF INCIDENCE, 2"

FIN

PAPER HERE

4"

7" 10"

36"

5"

4"

6"

16"

14"

32"

45"

METHOD OF CUTTING BAMBOO FOR JOINTS

ADJUSTABLE HITCH

CEMENTED AND LASHED

6" R.

12"

Pegless Sun Tent Erected Easily In Yard for Children

ROLLED UP

SHARP-POINTED STAKES IN HEMS

To avoid any possibility of a small child being injured by falling over pegs used to support a play sun tent, stitch hems in the ends of the cloth to receive four pointed sticks so that the tent may be erected as shown. The absence of both center poles and pegs makes such a tent especially suitable for small children. It is easy to erect or take down, and takes very little space when rolled for storage.

Snap-On Wings for Model Planes Are Less Likely to Be Broken

SNAPS ON WING AND STRUT

GLUED TO FUSELAGE

Model airplane wings are much less apt to be smashed when the plane strikes an object or makes a poor landing if they are attached to the fuselage with ordinary dress snaps, which will allow the wings to pull away from the fuselage without damage. One half of each snap should be glued to the wing and strut ends, and the matching halves glued to the correct locations on the fuselage. Allow the first coating of glue to set until thoroughly dry; then reinforce with more glue. The fuselage should be made somewhat stronger to take the added strain, but the extra weight will not be enough to interfere with flight. For carrying or for storage the easily removable wings also prove handy.

—Lynn Christensen, Long Beach, Calif.

Empty Match Book on a Wire Provides Air-Rifle Target

A target for air-rifle practice can be made by clipping an empty match book to a wire stretched between two supports. As these books are usually waxed, they will deflect the shot and spin if hit.

GET THE AXIS

BUY WAR BONDS

Six-Prong Fork of Twisted Wire Roasts Wieners Uniformly

Roasting six wieners at a time is easy for one camper who uses a fork shaped like the spokes of a wheel. It is made by twisting six lengths of wire together, fit-

KINKED PRONGS

WOODEN HANDLE

TWISTED WIRE

ting a wooden handle on one end and bending the opposite ends at right angles to the handle. By rotating the fork, all wieners are roasted uniformly as the escaping liquid flows down on the opposite ones and bastes them. It's a good idea to kink the prongs to prevent the wieners from slipping off into the fire.

"POWER MOUSE"—

BICYCLE GOOSENECK
BRAZED TO LONG
STEEL TUBE

SPONGE-
RUBBER
PAD

8½"

15⅝"

NO.81 CHAIN
42" LONG

BENDS
OVER LOWER
CROSS MEMBER
OF FORK

DURALUMIN
FENDER

6"

19½"

8¾"

18"

17"

1¼"TUBING

⅞"TUBING

12" BALLOON
WHEELS

8"

8½"

49"

①

Low center of gravity, flexible
chassis and positive chain drive
give speed with safety

⅞" OAK CHASSIS

3"

DUE to its exceptional simplicity, building this motor scooter is no lengthy, tedious job. The chassis is nothing more than a sturdy oak board, which was selected instead of a channel or angle-steel frame because it absorbs road shocks not taken up by the tires. The brake is applied by a lever on the handle bar and has sufficient power to slide the road wheel with only a moderate pressure. There is no clutch. The wooden hood over the power unit aids in silencing the engine and drive and directs heat and fumes out the rear.

Figs. 1 and 2 give the general dimensions while the underside of the chassis is illustrated in Fig. 3. Note that flat-iron plates are used where bolts come through the bottom, reinforcing the structure with a negligible addition of weight.

In construction, make the oak chassis first. The type of engine used may make some alteration necessary but on the original, cross cleats are bolted at each end of the chassis, a built-up block installed for the engine base and angle brackets made to serve as rear axle mounts. The right-

Speedy Motor Scooter

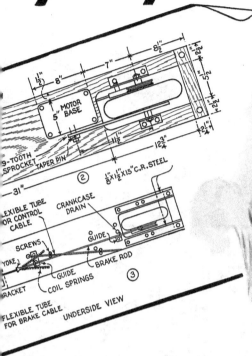

MOTOR BASE

9-TOOTH SPROCKET TAPER PIN

²⁄₈" x 1½" x 15" C.R. STEEL

FLEXIBLE TUBE FOR CONTROL CABLE CRANKCASE DRAIN

SCREWS GUIDE

YOKE BRAKE ROD

BRACKET GUIDE COIL SPRINGS

FLEXIBLE TUBE FOR BRAKE CABLE UNDERSIDE VIEW

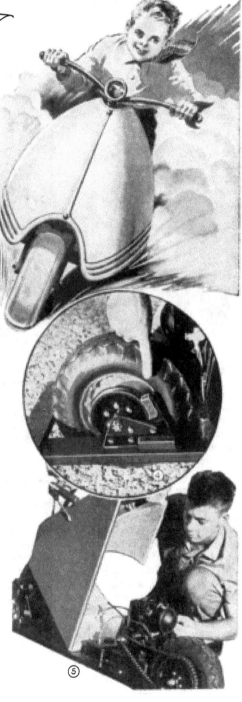

hand bracket is longer to carry the pivot bolt for the brake shoe. This brake, Figs. 4 and 7, is a hardwood block with a portion trimmed to fit into the V-groove of the brake pulley and covered with medium-weight leather. A strip of flat iron is bolted to the lower end of the block, providing a hanger to which the brake rod is connected. It is carried through guides, Fig. 6, and at the forward end two coil springs are connected to hold the shoe away from the pulley. A cable is carried through a flexible tube to the hand lever on the handle bar, Fig. 10. This latter equipment is from the braking assembly of a bicycle.

For the steering-post support three lengths of steel tubing, such as that used in a motorcycle frame, are welded to a heavier tube, as in Figs. 9 and 10. The angle of the tube A with the chassis should not exceed 30°. The fork is assembled as shown, with tubing from a motorcycle fork. The members B, Fig. 10, are flattened at the ends and drilled for the axle, and, with the tube D, are welded to the cross mem-

Labels in the diagram (right side):

SPONGE-RUBBER CUSHION

½" PLYWOOD
¾" PINE

18"
11"
8½"
6"
10½"
RIGHT SIDE OF HOOD
10"
⑦
BRAKE SHOE
GUIDE
LEATHER FACIN
2"OAK
16½"
BRAKE ROD
½"S
3/16 BC
CHOKE CONTROL
6"
3/16 X 32½" ROD
BOLT FOR BRAKE SHOE
1" CRANKCASE DRAIN
GAS TANK HERE
RIGHT
⅛" IRON
7"
LEFT
7/8"   2½"   7/8"
⅜"C.R.S. S.A.E. 18
LOCK NUTS
6½"
VEE PULLEY FOR BRAKE DRUM
FRONT-AXLE ASSEMBLY
12"X3" WHEEL
TYPE A, 45-TOOTH HUBLESS SPROCKET
COLLAR
9/16"
SPACERS WHEEL BOLT
¼" S.A.E.
DRIVE SPROCKET
SPACERS ON BOLTS
⑧ REAR-AXLE ASSEMBLY
S.A.E. 18
6⅞"
9/16"
5⅜"
REAR WHEEL BOL SPROCKET & VEE
SPACER SLEEVE

ber C. In welding part C to D, weld only on the upper side, as a ball-bearing cone is fitted on the underside of C, and the rough spots left by welding would interfere with a neat fit. Steel plugs ground or turned to a force fit are driven in the top ends of the two tubes B, a hole being drilled and tapped in each plug for the bolt which is to hold the cross member E in place. A duralumin front fender is made as detailed in Fig. 1. This is a very simple but entirely satisfactory job. For the steering post, Fig. 10, a length of ⅞-in. tubing is brazed to a bicycle gooseneck, slotted at the bottom and a long bolt made to screw into an expansion plug.

The front axle, shown in Fig. 8, consists of a rod, passing through a sleeve. This construction permits the assembly to be dismounted easily by unscrewing one of the nuts on the smaller axle. Ball-bearing wheels with 12x3-in. pneumatic tires, proved just the right size. As the rims are in two halves, bolted together, the original bolts are removed and 6¼-in. rods, cut to length and threaded on each end, are substituted. Sleeves cut from heavy tubing fit over the ends of the rods on both sides of the wheel. See the sectional view of the road wheel in Fig. 8. These sleeves space the sprocket and V-pulley so that both clear the tire. The wheels ride upon a stationary axle provided with one loose collar, and one integral collar as in Fig. 8.

For all-around service a 5-to-1 gear ratio is satisfactory. With a ½-hp. engine running at 2,000 r.p.m., the speed of the scooter on the level is about 17 m.p.h. For hilly sections, install a 6 or even a 7-to-1 ratio. The driven sprocket is of the hubless type with a bore large enough to clear the axle. For a 5-to-1 ratio, the driven sprocket should have 45 teeth, and the driving sprocket 9 teeth. The driving sprocket must have a hub on one side bored to fit the projecting end of the engine crankshaft. It should be keyed to the shaft. Use a No. 82 roller chain to drive. This arrangement

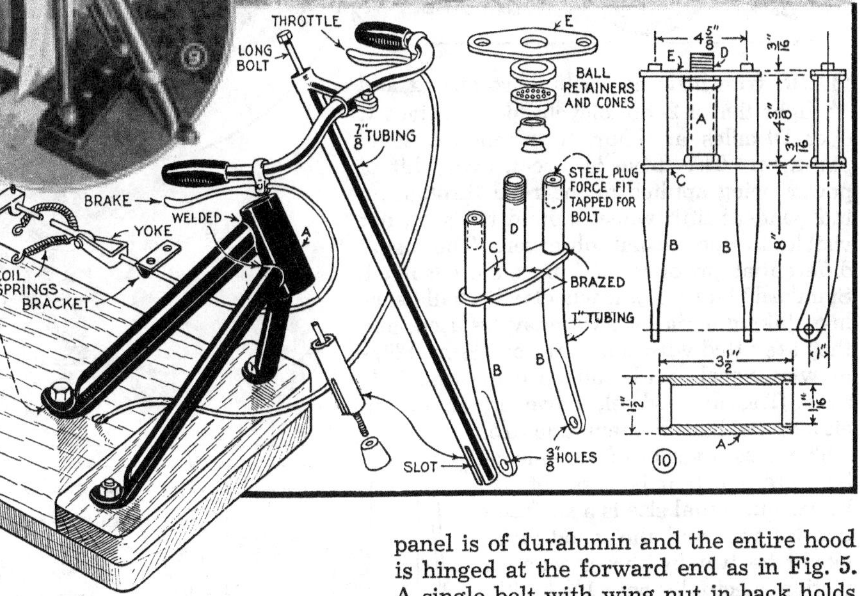

THROTTLE
LONG BOLT
BRAKE
YOKE
WELDED
GUIDE BOLTS
UNDERSIDE OF CHASSIS
COIL SPRINGS
BRACKET
⅞"TUBING
SLOT
E
E
D
BALL RETAINERS AND CONES
A
STEEL PLUG FORCE FIT TAPPED FOR BOLT
C
D
BRAZED
1"TUBING
B B
B B
⅜"HOLES
4⅝"
3 5/16"
4⅜"
3 3/16"
8"
3½"
1½"
1 1/16"
1"
A
⑨
⑩

eliminates many complications involved in a clutch or jackshaft drive. Direct drive proved more satisfactory because a slight push starts the motor, and in stopping the latter acts as a drag as soon as it is shut down, stopping the scooter more quickly than if the engine were de-clutched.

A wooden hood, Fig. 7, is easier to construct, more quiet and more satisfactory than a metal one. No great heat is accumulated inside because the engine fan carries it out back, along with exhaust fumes. Vents can be cut in the back of the hood for added circulation if desired. The rear panel is of duralumin and the entire hood is hinged at the forward end as in Fig. 5. A single bolt with wing nut in back holds it in place. Note that the choke is installed in the front panel near the floor, Fig. 7, but the builder can place it anywhere he finds convenient. The gas tank is bolted to the floor in front of the engine, and batteries for lights can also be installed under the hood if lamps without self-contained batteries are used.

Chinese red and black make a good color combination and can be seen readily by motorists. A natural wood finish on the oak chassis is attractive. Tail and head lamps can be had at reasonable cost at any bicycle shop.

35

BICYCLE *Runs* MIDGET

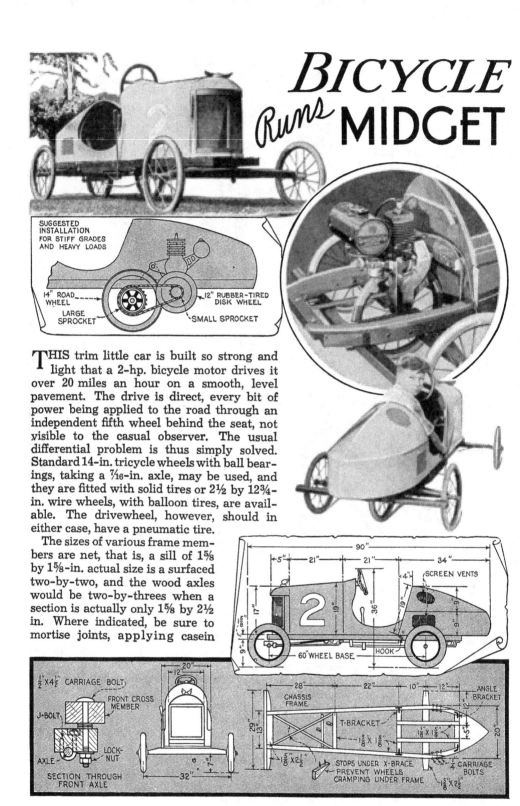

SUGGESTED INSTALLATION FOR STIFF GRADES AND HEAVY LOADS

14" ROAD WHEEL

LARGE SPROCKET

12" RUBBER-TIRED DISK WHEEL

SMALL SPROCKET

THIS trim little car is built so strong and light that a 2-hp. bicycle motor drives it over 20 miles an hour on a smooth, level pavement. The drive is direct, every bit of power being applied to the road through an independent fifth wheel behind the seat, not visible to the casual observer. The usual differential problem is thus simply solved. Standard 14-in. tricycle wheels with ball bearings, taking a 7/16-in. axle, may be used, and they are fitted with solid tires or 2½ by 12¾-in. wire wheels, with balloon tires, are available. The drivewheel, however, should in either case, have a pneumatic tire.

The sizes of various frame members are net, that is, a sill of 1⅝ by 1⅝-in. actual size is a surfaced two-by-two, and the wood axles would be two-by-threes when a section is actually only 1⅝ by 2½ in. Where indicated, be sure to mortise joints, applying casein

90"
5" 21" 21" 34"
SCREEN VENTS
4"
17" 19" 36"
2
9"
60" WHEEL BASE
HOOK

½" X 4½" CARRIAGE BOLT
FRONT CROSS MEMBER
J-BOLT
LOCK-NUT
AXLE
SECTION THROUGH FRONT AXLE

20"
12"
32"
7¼"

28" 22" 10" 12"
ANGLE BRACKET
CHASSIS FRAME
29"
T-BRACKET
1⅝" X 1⅝"
1⅝" X 1⅝"
20"
1⅝" X 2½"
STOPS UNDER X-BRACE PREVENT WHEELS CRAMPING UNDER FRAME
¼" CARRIAGE BOLTS
1⅝" X 2½"

MOTOR RACER

By HI SIBLEY

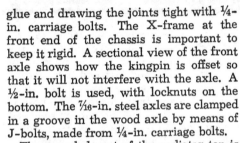

glue and drawing the joints tight with ¼-in. carriage bolts. The X-frame at the front end of the chassis is important to keep it rigid. A sectional view of the front axle shows how the kingpin is offset so that it will not interfere with the axle. A ½-in. bolt is used, with locknuts on the bottom. The 7/16-in. steel axles are clamped in a groove in the wood axle by means of J-bolts, made from ¼-in. carriage bolts.

The rounded part of the radiator top is built up of four pieces of ¾-in. stock glued together, with a fifth piece slightly smaller on the underside. The corners are rounded with drawshave, plane, rasp and sandpaper, then given a coat of filler and paint. The bottom consists of two pieces of wood, with a dowel-brace near the front of the curve and a pair of triangular supports at the back. When the car is assembled and painted, a heavy brass screen is tacked around the curves. A radiator cap from a wrecking yard completes the job.

After searching vainly for a 12-in. steer-

STEERING-GEAR DETAIL

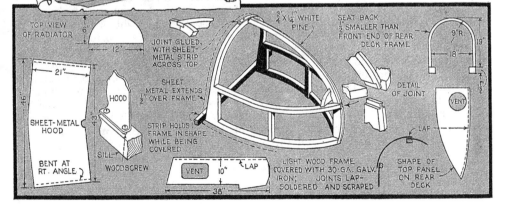

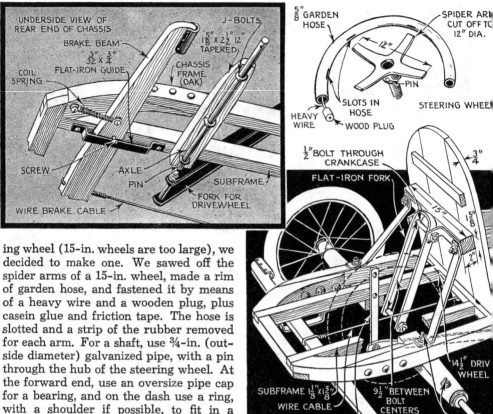

UNDERSIDE VIEW OF REAR END OF CHASSIS
BRAKE BEAM
$\frac{3}{32}$ X $\frac{3}{4}$
FLAT-IRON GUIDE
COIL SPRING
CHASSIS FRAME (OAK)
J-BOLTS
$1\frac{5}{8}$" X $2\frac{1}{2}$" 12" TAPERED
SCREW
AXLE
PIN
SUBFRAME
FORK FOR DRIVEWHEEL
WIRE BRAKE CABLE

$\frac{5}{8}$" GARDEN HOSE
SPIDER ARM CUT OFF TO 12" DIA.
12"
PIN
SLOTS IN HOSE
HEAVY WIRE
WOOD PLUG
STEERING WHEEL

$\frac{1}{2}$" BOLT THROUGH CRANKCASE
$\frac{3}{4}$
FLAT-IRON FORK
15"
$1\frac{5}{8}$"
2$\frac{1}{2}$"
$14\frac{1}{2}$" DRIVE WHEEL
SUBFRAME $1\frac{1}{8}$"X$1\frac{5}{8}$"
WIRE CABLE
$\frac{1}{8}$"X$\frac{7}{8}$"X12" ARM BOLTS TO MUFFLER TO RAISE MOTOR OFF WHEEL
$9\frac{1}{2}$" BETWEEN BOLT CENTERS
J-BOLTS
BRAKE BEAM 1"X3"X35"
SPLIT HOSE

ing wheel (15-in. wheels are too large), we decided to make one. We sawed off the spider arms of a 15-in. wheel, made a rim of garden hose, and fastened it by means of a heavy wire and a wooden plug, plus casein glue and friction tape. The hose is slotted and a strip of the rubber removed for each arm. For a shaft, use ¾-in. (outside diameter) galvanized pipe, with a pin through the hub of the steering wheel. At the forward end, use an oversize pipe cap for a bearing, and on the dash use a ring, with a shoulder if possible, to fit in a notch in the top of the dash. The ring may be held in place by two screws over the edge. The dash should be strengthened by four cleats on the inside to prevent splitting, for it must be arched to admit the knees of the pilot. The drum on the steering column is of wood, 3 in. in diameter and 5 in. long, and is pinned to the shaft with a spike. A good grade of sash cord is used for the cable and is first stretched by towing some load behind a car. The cables should leave the drum at right angles to the axle, or they will climb one way or another and bunch up. The pulleys can be located to give desired results, and also so that the driver can slide his legs on either side of the cords. Fasten the ends to heavy screweyes in the wood axle, each 9 in. from the kingpin. On one cable end, install a stiff coil tension spring, and on the other a snaphook and turnbuckle.

The original job is powered with a standard bicycle motor, which has a friction pulley that rides on the tire. The installation is very simple, the motor being applied in the same manner as on the bicycle. A heavy cleat is fastened to the back of the seat with carriage bolts, and is further braced by two heavy flat-iron bars to the chassis frame. A stout iron fork swings in a yoke just the right size to receive the motor, which is supported by a bolt through the forward end of the cranckcase. The drivewheel also rides in this fork, which is held only by the bolt through the upper end and thus rides all irregularities of the road entirely independent of the car. A vertical arm is bolted to one side of the muffler of this motor, connected at the bottom to a tie-rod, running to the clutch lever which lifts the motor off the wheel when stopping, idling or warming up. No alterations or machine work are necessary to install the motor. The fork

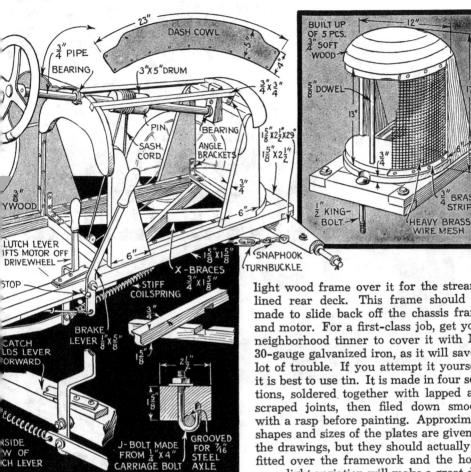

Figure labels (illustration):

- 23"
- DASH COWL
- 3/4" PIPE BEARING
- 3"X 5"DRUM
- 3/4"X 3/4"
- BUILT UP OF 5 PCS. 3/4" SOFT WOOD
- 12"
- 5/8" DOWEL
- 17"
- 13"
- PIN
- BEARING
- SASH CORD
- ANGLE BRACKETS
- 1 5/8"X2 1/2"X29"
- 1 5/8"X2 1/2"
- 3/4"
- 3/4"
- 3/8" PLYWOOD
- 3/4" BRASS STRIP
- 1/2" KING BOLT
- HEAVY BRASS WIRE MESH
- CLUTCH LEVER LIFTS MOTOR OFF DRIVEWHEEL
- 6"
- 6"
- STOP
- STIFF COILSPRING
- X-BRACES
- 3/4"X1 5/8"
- 1 5/8"X1 5/8"
- SNAPHOOK
- TURNBUCKLE
- 3/4"
- BRAKE LEVER 1/8"X 5/8"
- 1 5/8"
- 2 1/2"
- 1 5/8"
- INSIDE VIEW OF CATCH LEVER
- CATCH HOLDS LEVER FORWARD
- J-BOLT MADE FROM 1/4"X 4" CARRIAGE BOLT
- GROOVED FOR 7/16" STEEL AXLE

which carries the drivewheel is, however, special and should be made to specifications to insure rigidity. The so-called clutch lever is provided with a catch. A heavy coil spring on this lever holds the motor down on the wheel and prevents bouncing. To start the car, the pilot simply pushes it, with the clutch engaged, a few feet, then lifts off the motor and climbs in. Of course, one should not expect to start up grades or on rough roads in this manner.

Here is a very simple braking arrangement which will lock rear wheels with little effort. The shoes are split sections of garden hose nailed to a wood beam held away from the wheels by a pair of coil springs. A wire cable, guided through screweyes to a brake lever, completes it.

After the motor is installed, build the light wood frame over it for the streamlined rear deck. This frame should be made to slide back off the chassis frame and motor. For a first-class job, get your neighborhood tinner to cover it with No. 30-gauge galvanized iron, as it will save a lot of trouble. If you attempt it yourself, it is best to use tin. It is made in four sections, soldered together with lapped and scraped joints, then filed down smooth with a rasp before painting. Approximate shapes and sizes of the plates are given in the drawings, but they should actually be fitted over the framework and the hood, as a slight variation will make a great difference in sheet-metal work. The open panels in the rear deck have galvanized fly screen soldered on the inside. Aluminum would make a nice light job but is more expensive and difficult to solder.

In case you expect to carry heavier loads than the average, or negotiate stiff grades or rough roads, a suggestion is shown for a geared-down ratio, wherein the motor drives the road wheel indirectly through a friction wheel plus sprockets and chain. In this case you will not attain as high speed as in direct drive, and it may be necessary to install a small cooling fan on the motor. Another means of increasing the power ratio is to substitute a smaller friction pulley on the motor. The standard pulley is 3 in. in diameter, but a 2½ or 2¼-in. pulley would greatly increase its pulling ability. This, of course, would be a special machine job.

"Sea-Bee"

a gas-driven Model Speedboat

By Floyd M. Mix

THIS 32-in. motorboat, designed by F. E. Ludolph, of Chicago, is powered by a 22-oz. midget gas engine that develops approximately ⅓ hp. at 5,000 r.p.m., and drives the boat on a circular course at a speed of 30 to 35 m.p.h. The job of building the boat is not difficult if the directions are carefully followed. The thrills of racing it will more than compensate you for your work in finishing this project.

Assuming that all of the items specified in the material list at the end of this article are at hand, let's get right into the constructional details. The frames dimensioned on print No. 965 are made from birch plywood, Nos. 1, 3, 5 and transom from ⅜-in. stock and Nos. 2 and 6 from ¾-in. stock. To obtain full-size patterns of the frames, rule sheets of kraft paper into 1-in. squares, then sketch the patterns of the half frames given in the small squares into the large ones freehand. Fold the paper along the center line with the pattern on the outside and cut along this line with a pair of scissors to make both sides symmetrical. Then you fasten the patterns on the plywood, using rubber ce-

ment, and scroll-saw the frames to shape, Fig. 7. Cut the nose block from a piece of birch or white pine 2 by 3 by 6 in. in size. Carve the block to approximate shape and

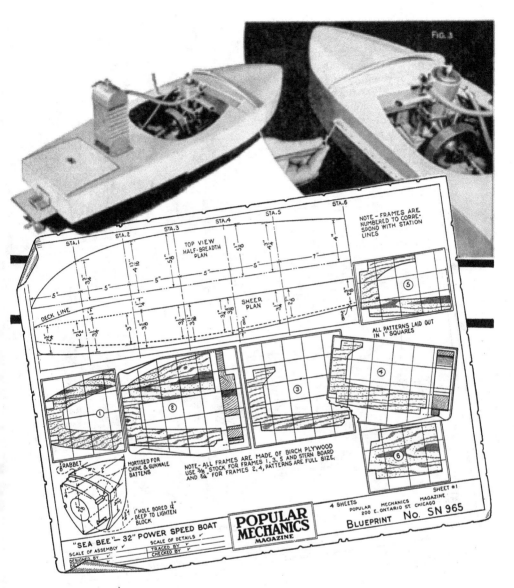

Fig. 3

NOTE – FRAMES ARE NUMBERED TO CORRESPOND WITH STATION LINES

STA.1 STA.2 STA.3 STA.4 STA.5 STA.6

TOP VIEW HALF-BREADTH PLAN

DECK LINE

SHEER PLAN

⑤

ALL PATTERNS LAID OUT IN 1" SQUARES

④

③

②

①

⑥

NOTE – ALL FRAMES ARE MADE OF BIRCH PLYWOOD USE 3/8" STOCK FOR FRAMES 1, 3, 5 AND STERN BOARD AND 3/4" FOR FRAMES 2, 4, PATTERNS ARE FULL SIZE.

RABBET

MORTISED FOR CHINE & GUNWALE BATTENS

1" HOLE BORED 4" DEEP TO LIGHTEN BLOCK

SHEET #1

4 SHEETS   POPULAR   MECHANICS   MAGAZINE
200 E. ONTARIO ST. CHICAGO

BLUEPRINT No. SN 965

POPULAR MECHANICS MAGAZINE

"SEA BEE" – 32" POWER SPEED BOAT

SCALE OF DETAILS
SCALE OF ASSEMBLY
DESIGNED BY
DRAWN BY
TRACED BY
CHECKED BY

rabbet it ⅛ in. as indicated. Also, rabbet frames 2 and 4 as shown in the end view of these pieces.

The framework, Fig. 10, is assembled on a building board or form, the upper side of which is cut to the contour indicated in Fig. 4. Aside from temporary nailing required to fasten the frame pieces to the form, all parts of the model are fastened in place with flat-head brass screws and waterproof casein or marine glue. Also, all of the wood surface must be shellacked and given a couple coats of marine paint of the desired shade to protect it from the mois-

ture. Naturally this must be done as the work progresses otherwise part of the inner works would be inaccessible.

Now to get started with the assembling: The keel is fastened to the nose block and then to the building form as shown in Fig. 5. The frames are placed in their respective positions as indicated in the half-breadth plan, print No. 965, and toenailed in place with 1-in. wire brads. Both chine and deck beams are ⅜ in. square, being ripped from a piece of clear white pine about 36 in. long. These pieces are heated thoroughly over a gas burner so they will bend without breaking, then fastened to the frames with glue and No. 4 f. h. brass screws, ⅝ in. long. The heads are countersunk to allow for evening up the frames in preparation for the planking. All planking is ⅛-in. birch plywood, and it is glued and screwed to the frame pieces with No. 0, ⅜-in. f. h. brass screws. To avoid waste of material and to aid in getting the plywood shaped properly, it is a good idea to make up cardboard patterns of the various pieces required. Where necessary, the

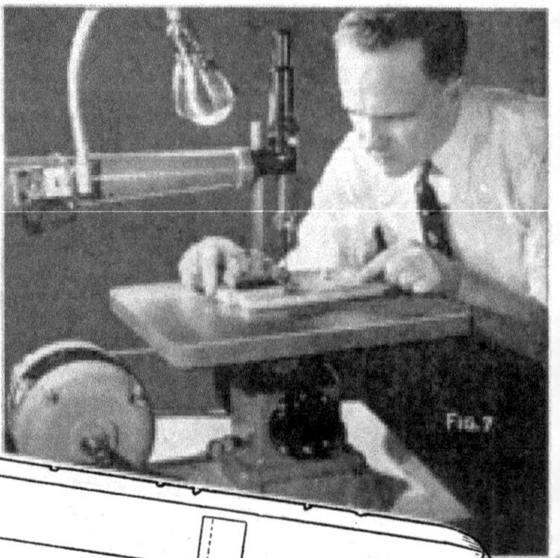
FIG. 7

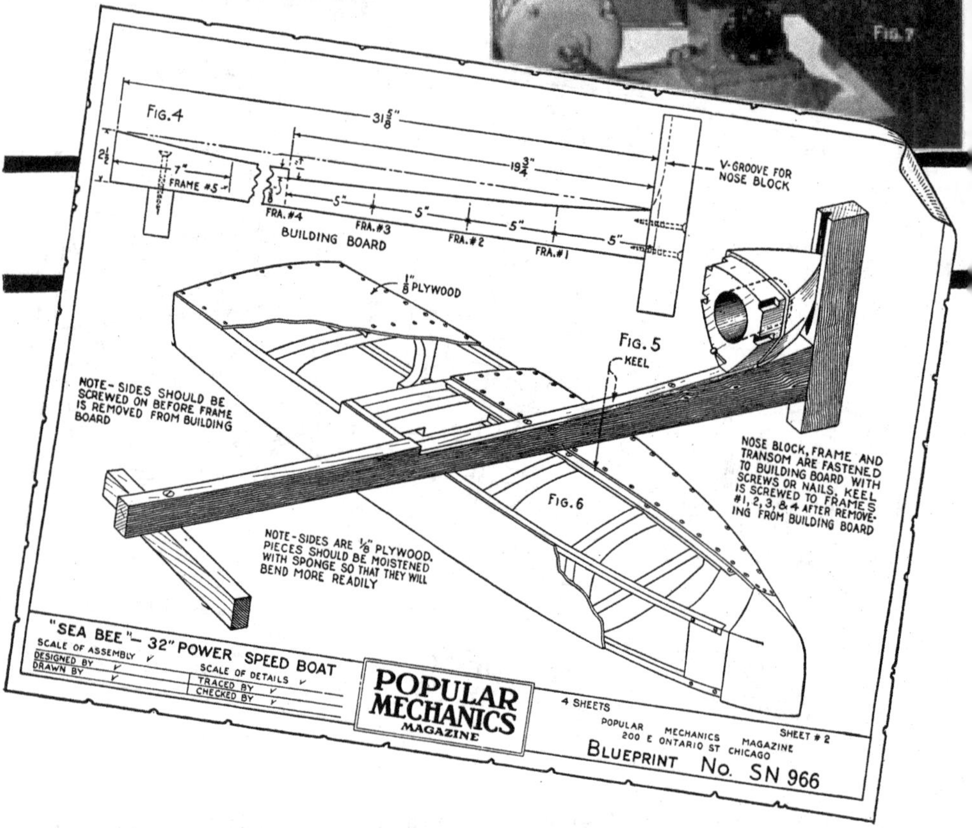

FIG. 4
31⅝"
2½"
7"
FRAME #5
19¾"
V-GROOVE FOR NOSE BLOCK
5"
5"
5"
5"
FRA. #4
FRA. #3
FRA. #2
FRA. #1
BUILDING BOARD
⅛" PLYWOOD
FIG. 5
KEEL
NOTE- SIDES SHOULD BE SCREWED ON BEFORE FRAME IS REMOVED FROM BUILDING BOARD
NOSE BLOCK, FRAME AND TRANSOM ARE FASTENED TO BUILDING BOARD WITH SCREWS OR NAILS. KEEL IS SCREWED TO FRAMES #1, 2, 3, & 4 AFTER REMOVING FROM BUILDING BOARD
FIG. 6
NOTE-SIDES ARE ⅛" PLYWOOD. PIECES SHOULD BE MOISTENED WITH SPONGE SO THAT THEY WILL BEND MORE READILY
"SEA BEE"- 32" POWER SPEED BOAT
SCALE OF ASSEMBLY
SCALE OF DETAILS
DESIGNED BY
DRAWN BY
TRACED BY
CHECKED BY
POPULAR MECHANICS MAGAZINE
4 SHEETS
SHEET # 2
POPULAR MECHANICS MAGAZINE 200 E ONTARIO ST CHICAGO
BLUEPRINT No. SN 966

frames are dressed down with a rasp to insure a good fit at all joints. After all the frames have been attached, the side planks are put on. Contacting surfaces are smeared with glue and C-clamps used to hold the wood in place until the screws are driven in. About four screws, staggered to prevent splitting, will be required for each frame piece. After both side planks are in place, the model is removed from the form and the keel is fastened to frames 1, 2, 3, and 4. Fig. 6 shows details on the bottom planking. By sponging the pieces with warm water, they can be bent readily to the contour of the framework.

Now build a cradle for the model from ¾-in. plywood, as shown in Fig. 18. The motor base, Fig. 9, and the drive-shaft support just ahead of frame No. 4, come next. A battery compartment, which accommodates the four flashlight cells required to operate the engine, is illustrated in Fig. 16. When the battery compartment is in place and a cover made for it, as dimensioned in

As soon as all of the drive-shaft mechanism is lined up, you can go ahead with the deck planking, Fig. 11. Start with the forward deck, covering it with ½-in. strips of ⅛-in. plywood. Put on the middle plank first, then gradually work toward the sides. The aft deck is covered with a piece of the same material, openings being cut in it as shown in Fig. 13. On print No. 967, Fig. 12, you will find dimensions for the windshield and mold-

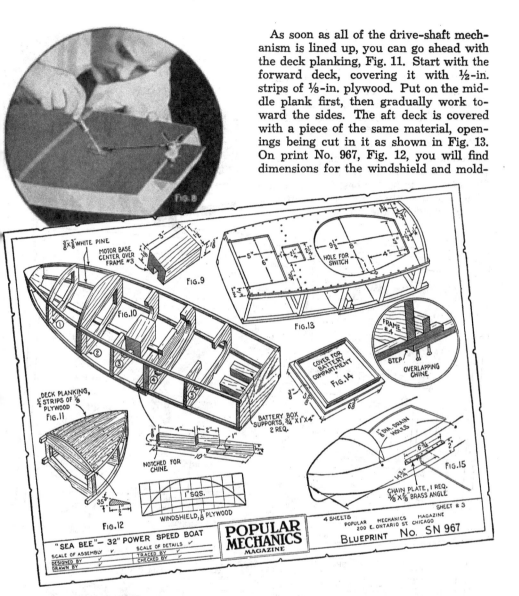

Fig. 14, you can go ahead with the preliminary wiring, using small staples to anchor the wires to the side of one of the deck beams. Notch the top edge of the frames where necessary. Be sure the wires are left long enough to make all the necessary connections after the engine has been installed and the top decking applied. Refer to Figs. 8, 17, 19 and 20 for data on the drive-shaft and propeller installation. To provide a thrust bearing for the propeller shaft, slip a ¾-in. length of ¼-in. brass tubing over it and solder it in place just back of the bearing.

ing to which it is attached. With the windshield on, the main construction is finished, but there's still several odd jobs to clear up. A radio plug must be installed in the forward deck, Fig. 1, so you can use an auxiliary battery for starting, and a switch, detailed in Fig. 16, mounted on the aft deck, to stop the engine at the close of a race. Then there's the chain plate, Figs. 3 and 15, and the installation of the motor, Fig. 2, radiator, and 1½-in. propeller. For the outside finish on the boat use a coat of thin shellac, and a couple coats of marine paint of the desired shade, sanding lightly between coats. When ready for a trial run, the model is placed on the cradle and the engine started by twisting the propeller as in Fig. 21. Speed is controlled by adjusting the carburetor needle valve, spark and choke valve before placing the model in the water. A tank of fuel will run the motor from 15 to 20 min.

For a circular race course the boat is attached to a 50-ft. line which pivots on a pole not over 4 ft. above the water level. The model making the best time in a race of not less than three consecutive circular laps is considered the winner.

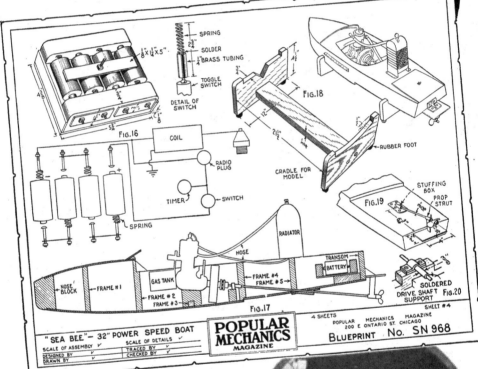

A TWIST OF THE PROPELLER STARTS THE ENGINE

FIG. 21

MATERIAL LIST

1 pc. ⅜x24x36-in. birch plywood—frames
1 pc. ¾x12x12-in. birch plywood—frames
1 pc. ¾x18x24-in. birch plywood—cradle, battery box
1 pc. 2x3x4-in. birch—nose block
1 pc. ⅜x3x36-in. white pine—chines, deck beams
2 pc. ⅛x24x36-in. birch plywood—planking, windshield
1 pc. 2x4x12-in. white pine—motor base, miscellaneous
1 pc. brass angle ⅜x⅝x6¾ in.—chain plate
1 pc. 3/16-in. steel rod approx. 20 in. long—drive shaft
1½ lbs. No. 0, f. h. brass screws ⅝ in. long
Universal joint, prop strut, stuffing box, shaft bearing, propeller
Marine glue, several sizes of wire brads and screws

Midget GAS ENGINE

weighs only four ounces

Two-cycle operation reduces moving parts to the minimum, making it an easy lathe job

HERE'S one of the smallest practical gas engines ever built—½-in. bore and a ⅝-in. stroke. Designed by three well-known model builders, Victor Savage, Erwin Schwartz and R. H. Barney, it has successfully flown a tiny monoplane whose total weight was only 17 oz., including the engine.

The cylinder is made from steel tubing ⅞ in. in diameter with a ³⁄₁₆-in. wall. This leaves a ½-in. bore, which should be reamed after chucking in the lathe. The first lathe operation is turning and threading the lower end which is to be screwed into the crankcase. Finished

EXHAUST STROKE

INTAKE STROKE

½"

⅞"

OPERATION DETAILS ③

ALL PORTS TWO ³⁄₃₂" HOLES SIDE BY SIDE EXCEPT AS INDICATED

THREADED FOR STANDARD MODEL AIRPLANE PLUG

EXHAUST

³⁄₃₂ HOLES

BY-PASS

INTAKE

#32 THREAD ② LOCATING PORTS

1" BORE

INTAKE MANIFOLD BRAZED ON

#32 THREAD

CYLINDER ④

to turn and thread the top where the head is to be screwed on and fifth, cut the cylinder to length with the parting tool. Before drilling the ports study the operation diagram, Fig. 3, which shows how the piston clears the ports in one position and closes them in another. Dimensions for locating port centers are given in Fig. 2. When these are drilled, as in Fig. 13, the cold-rolled sheet-steel manifold is brazed on the cylinder over the by-pass ports. See Fig. 12. At this stage the cylinder should be

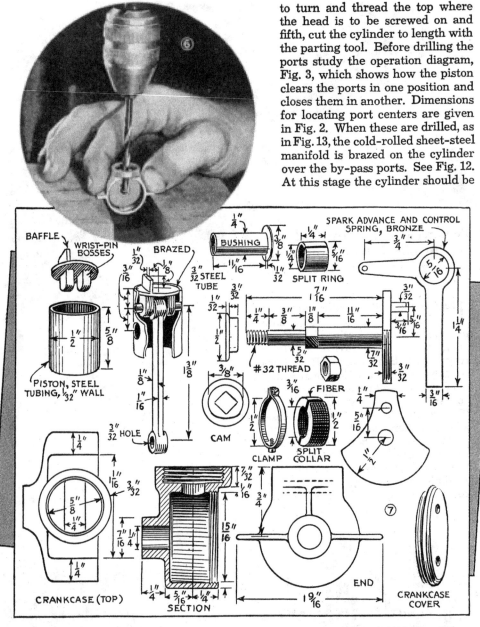

dimensions of the cylinder are given in Fig. 4. The second operation is to turn down that section of the cylinder between the base and fins. The latter are only $\frac{1}{64}$ in. thick, and the space between them is $\frac{1}{16}$ in. wide so you will need a $\frac{1}{16}$-in. parting or cutting-off tool to do this job, Figs. 5 and 17. There are nine fins on the cylinder and three on the head. The fourth operation is

hardened by heating to 1,600° F. and dropping in water. The degree of heat can be determined by checking its color with that of a chart. Next is lapping and polishing the bore. Turn a brass rod to a sliding fit in the cylinder. Cut two grooves as shown to carry abrasive. Chuck the rod and apply grade-A lapping compound in the grooves, Fig. 11. Start the lathe and slip the cylinder over the rod, holding it in the hand and working back and forth. As soon as the cylinder slides freely on the revolving rod and has taken on a high polish, it is finished.

The cylinder head is turned from a solid bar of ⅞-in. cold-rolled steel as in Fig. 18. Bore the large and small inside diameters, Fig. 4, and then cut the threads and fins, and finally cut off to exact length. The head need not be hardened or polished but make sure that it seats true on the top of the cylinder, as no gasket is used.

Steel tubing, ⁹⁄₁₆ in. in diameter with a ⅛-in. wall makes the pis-

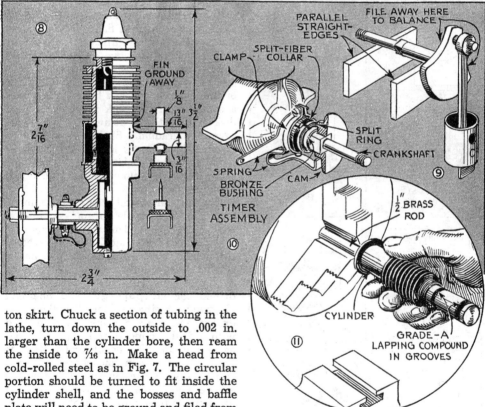

ton skirt. Chuck a section of tubing in the lathe, turn down the outside to .002 in. larger than the cylinder bore, then ream the inside to ⁷⁄₁₆ in. Make a head from cold-rolled steel as in Fig. 7. The circular portion should be turned to fit inside the cylinder shell, and the bosses and baffle plate will need to be ground and filed from the solid if you have no milling equipment. Braze in the head, drill for wrist pin and port, Fig. 14, and then harden by the same process as used for the cylinder. A groove should be cut at the base of the piston to make it easier to cut off after hardening.

Chuck the piston in the lathe and grind with a tool-post grinder until it can just be started into the cylinder, after which it should be lapped in to a close, but free-moving fit.

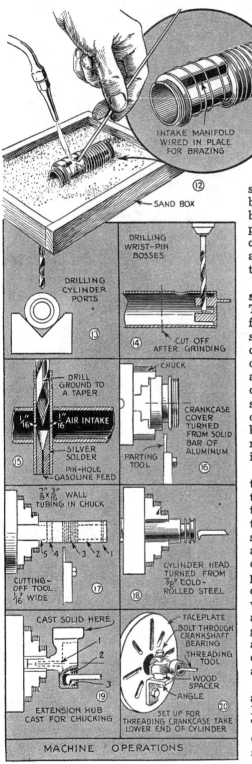

INTAKE MANIFOLD
WIRED IN PLACE
FOR BRAZING

⑫

← SAND BOX

DRILLING
CYLINDER
PORTS

DRILLING
WRIST-PIN
BOSSES

⑬

⑭ CUT OFF
AFTER GRINDING

DRILL
GROUND TO
A TAPER

CHUCK

1" / 16   1" / 16 AIR INTAKE

CRANKCASE
COVER
TURNED
FROM SOLID
BAR OF
ALUMINUM

SILVER
SOLDER

PARTING
TOOL

⑮

PIN-HOLE
GASOLINE FEED

⑯

7" / 8 3" / 16 WALL
TUBING IN CHUCK

5 4   3 2 1

CUTTING-
OFF TOOL
1" / 16 WIDE

⑰

CYLINDER HEAD
TURNED FROM
7/8" COLD-
ROLLED STEEL

⑱

CAST SOLID HERE

FACEPLATE

BOLT THROUGH
CRANKSHAFT
BEARING

THREADING
TOOL

WOOD
SPACER

ANGLE

⑲

EXTENSION HUB
CAST FOR CHUCKING

⑳

SET UP FOR
THREADING CRANKCASE TAKE
LOWER END OF CYLINDER

MACHINE OPERATIONS

Make a wood pattern for the bronze connecting rod somewhat thicker than finished dimensions so that there will be enough stock for smoothing up and polishing with file and buffer. In making a pattern for the aluminum crankcase, Fig. 7, extend the crankshaft-bearing hub 1 in. so that it can be chucked for turning. No cores are used, the top section being cast solid, then drilled out as in Fig. 6. First bore the crankshaft bearing, turn the inside of the chamber, then thread, as shown in Fig. 19. To bore and thread the top for the cylinder proceed as in Fig. 20. A cover for the crankcase is turned from a solid bar of aluminum, as in Fig. 16, and cut off after threading.

Now a bronze bushing is turned from solid stock to a press fit in the crankcase. The crankshaft is turned from a drop-forged bar and has two diameters with a squared section between. See Fig. 7. The crank is a separate piece brazed on the end of the shaft, which has been turned with a shoulder. This crank is simply a steel disk with sections cut away with a hacksaw, then gradually filed down to balance on straightedges, as in Fig. 9. It should be so accurately balanced that it will remain in any position whether the crank is up or down.

After a trial assembly of all parts made thus far, disassemble so you can put on the mixing valve. This unit consists of a thin piece of 3/16-in. steel tubing brazed to the cylinder over the intake port, and a smaller tube running through it at right angles, as in Figs. 3 and 8. The latter is drilled for air passage, and one end plugged with silver solder. It is then pin-drilled and a needle-valve seat formed with a drill ground to the required taper as in Fig. 15. The needle valve itself is ground from a 1/16-in. phosphor-bronze rod and fitted with a screw cap. Note that the engine is mounted in an inverted position as shown in the photo above Fig. 1.

Now for the ignition assembly, Figs. 7 and 10. A square hole is filed in the cam, Fig. 7, and one section of the hub flattened. This permits the spring to make contact on a screw head, completing the circuit. A split collar is clamped tightly on the bronze hub to maintain spark timing. The split-fiber collar is clamped by the brass band to which the ignition wire is soldered.

As this engine is designed to operate at sustained high speeds, accurate machining and fitting of all moving parts is of the utmost importance. It is of equal importance that the piston and by-pass ports register perfectly at the bottom of the stroke. For this reason the thickness of the gasket between the cylinder and crankcase must be checked carefully. A thin gasket is also used under the crankcase cover. The standard model-airplane spark plug is already provided with a gasket. In testing the engine it should be mounted solidly, equipped with a 10-in. propeller, and the current supplied by two or three dry cells and a conventional coil. The large batteries will supply ample current until you get it down to a fine adjustment. Fountain-pen flashlight batteries will suffice after the engine has been mounted in a plane. Of course, it is understood that oil is mixed with the gasoline—about one-tenth volume oil.

False Lock Keeps Loiterers Out of Building

A contractor who stored heavy equipment in a shed near the job, found that it was inconvenient to keep the building locked, as several workers had to have access to the place and there were not enough keys for all. As the contents could not be stolen easily, but it was desired to keep loiterers out, he used a false lock, as shown. An ordinary hasp was used, and from this the hinge pin was removed and a loose pin substituted. The padlock was left locked in place and access gained by merely employing a nail to lift the hinge pin from the hasp.—G. E. Hendrickson, Argyle, Wis.

¶When a caster in a chair or couch becomes loose fill the hole with wood putty and insert the shank of the caster in it. When the putty hardens it will hold firmly.

Simplified Electric Motor Run by Magnets

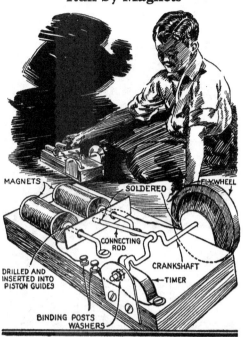

A dry cell and two electromagnets taken from a doorbell operate this motor

Operated on a dry cell, this engine runs at a fast clip, and is a real thriller to the young engineer because all the moving parts are exposed. Two electromagnets taken from a doorbell provide the pulling power to operate the "piston" which is a piece of heavy-gauge sheet iron soldered to a connecting rod and drilled to slide on two pieces of heavy wire. Two ends of the wires are bent and screwed to the base and the other ends are inserted into shallow holes drilled into the cores of the magnets. The connecting rod and crankshaft are made of heavy wire and the crankshaft has two throws, one for the connecting rod and one for the timer, which is a strip of copper. The flywheel is made of wood and the crank assembly is supported by two metal brackets which serve as bearings, the assembly being held in place by the flywheel on one side and a small washer soldered to the crankshaft on the other side. In setting the timer, it should be in contact with the crankshaft from the beginning of a stroke until the piston reaches the end of the stroke next to the magnets.

DECK PLAN

$1\frac{1}{2}''$

$3'\text{-}6''$

①

1"x6"x6'-0" PLYWOOD

60° SEGMENTS

UPRIGHTS $1\frac{1}{2}$ X 13"

$1\frac{1}{2}''$

GUNWALE PIECES

$\frac{3}{4}''$#6 BRASS OVAL-HEAD SCREWS & WASHERS, TOP AND BOTTOM

$\frac{1}{8}''$X15" HARD-PRESSED BOARD (TEMPERED)

$\frac{3}{4}''$X$1\frac{1}{2}''$ PINE

15"

BOTTOM, $\frac{3}{8}''$ PLYWOOD

②

$3'\text{-}9''$

BOTTOM

$\frac{5}{8}''$X$1\frac{1}{2}''$ PLYWOOD

15"

$\frac{1}{4}''$X6"X10" PLYWOOD

$\frac{3}{4}''$#6 BRASS OVAL HEAD SCREWS & WASHERS

$\frac{3}{4}''$X2" PINE

CHINE

DUCK-FOOT PADDLE

BRADS BENT OVER

CANDLE-WICKING LAID IN MARINE GLUE

BOTTOM

WATER

NO ONE in your beach party will be bored for want of something to do if you have several of these fun-making gadgets at hand. For example, there's racing with the circular craft shown above, called a "Coracle" after ancient European fishing boats. This tricky craft will provide no end of sport because of the difficulty in making it follow a straight course.

Just follow the details shown in Figs. 1 and 2. You'll want to duplicate the parts, of course, so that you will have two or more completed craft. The paddle is simply a piece of ¼-in. plywood with rubber loops for the fingers.

Then, there's "Skipperoo," strictly a water game and one that will revive memories of the fun you had as a youngster skipping flat stones across a pond. To play the game you need quiet water, a number of wooden disks, an old tennis net and a goal. The disks are turned from hardwood, making the bottom somewhat flatter than the top. Different colored disks are allotted to different players. Smooth the disk and give it a spar varnish or wax finish. The object is to skip the disk over the net into the boat.

If you like a little more adventure you

CIRCLE PAINTED
IN DIFFERENT
COLOR FOR
EACH PLAYER

—4" DIA.—
TURNED FROM
HARDWOOD ③

FINISHED
WITH SPAR
VARNISH

SPORTS

might try the "Sea Skis" detailed in Fig. 4. Two pontoons, linked in such a way that they are always parallel, enable one to "walk" about on smooth water.

Should you go in for log rolling, Fig. 5, you had best be prepared to swim a good share of the time. If you're an amateur at it, either you or someone else will have a lot of fun while you are learning. An artificial log can be made of a round galvanized tank covered with a wooden shell of battens bound with iron straps, as shown. Put the filler cap in the end so that buoyancy can be regulated by filling the tank with water. The log should float about three-quarters submerged. The tank must have three or more baffles inside to prevent the water ballast shifting too quickly. A satisfactory log also can be made by covering three or four Ford model-T gas tanks with battens and canvas. In this arrangement the water will need to be put in first and the tanks permanently sealed.

Another novelty is the "Tampa Tractor" detailed in Fig. 6, simply a light surfboard with a paddle wheel in front and a rudder which you control with your feet. When finished, the entire job should be painted or varnished carefully to prevent moisture

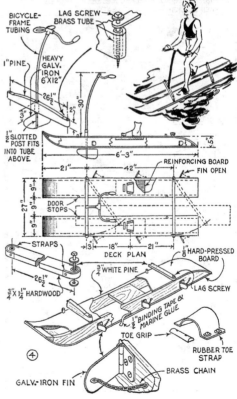

BICYCLE-
FRAME
TUBING

LAG SCREW
BRASS TUBE

1"PINE

HEAVY
GALV.
IRON
6"X12"

26½"

3"

30"

2"

1"SLOTTED
POST FITS
INTO TUBE
ABOVE

6'-3"

REINFORCING BOARD
FIN OPEN

21"

42"

27"
9"
9"
9"

DOOR
STOPS

STRAPS

3"
18"
21"

DECK PLAN

¼"HARD-PRESSED
BOARD

26½"

¾ WHITE PINE

¾"X1¼"HARDWOOD

④

5½"

LAG SCREW

1"BINDING TAPE &
½ MARINE GLUE

TOE GRIP

RUBBER TOE
STRAP

GALV.-IRON FIN

BRASS CHAIN

CANVAS TIGHTENED WITH AIRPLANE-FABRIC DOPE

GALV. IRON TANK
$\frac{3}{4}$"X1$\frac{1}{2}$" BATTENS
PERFORATED BAFFLES
GALV.IRON STRAP, BRASS SCREWS
BANDS
MODEL-T FORD GAS TANKS
FILLER CAP
SPACER BLOCKS
BATTENS

⑤

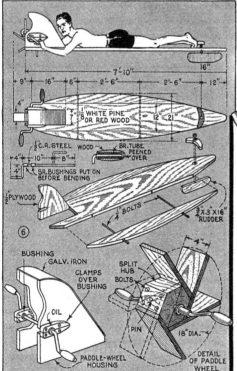

7'-10"
16"
9" 16" 6" 2'-6" 2'-6" 12"
$\frac{5}{8}$" WHITE PINE OR RED WOOD
12" 21"
$\frac{1}{2}$" C.R.STEEL WOOD
BR. TUBE PEENED OVER
4" 10" 8"
BR. BUSHINGS PUT ON BEFORE BENDING
$\frac{1}{2}$" PLYWOOD
1" BOLTS
$\frac{5}{8}$"X3"X16" RUDDER
⑥

BUSHING
GALV. IRON
SPLIT HUB
CLAMPS OVER BUSHING
BOLTS
OIL
PIN
18" DIA.
PADDLE-WHEEL HOUSING
DETAIL OF PADDLE WHEEL

from getting in and increasing its weight.

And now a child's rowboat with a novel feature, Fig. 7. No matter how awkward the young rower may be he cannot help but make the boat go forward for the oars are made to move in a vertical plane and the hinged blade pushes the water only on the power stroke—on the return stroke the blade swings free, causing a minimum of resistance. Make the hull of two side members of light wood such as white pine or redwood, with three cross-members on the bottom and end pieces. Turn this frame upside down and lay cotton binding tape along the edges of the side boards after applying marine glue liberally. Now lay on tempered hard-pressed board ⅛ in. thick and fasten with galvanized shingle nails, staggered and about 1 in. apart. This makes a permanently water-tight joint. A keel is bolted on later. The oars are of pine, with a short piece of brass tube for a bearing on the axis or "oarlock." The fin of heavy-gauge galvanized iron swings on a bolt and rests against a stop-pin on the power stroke.

Everybody likes to fish, of course, and there are many kinds of fish including those shown in Fig. 8. Along with the varieties detailed, you add a boot or tree branch to take care of over-confident anglers. The "fish" are weighted so that they submerge with only a wire loop floating above the surface. Fishermen use the regular tackle and a small lead weight for "bait." The trick, and it's not so easy, is to

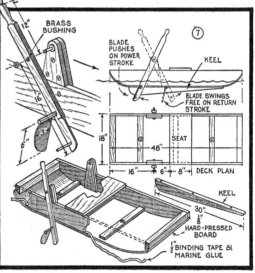

BRASS BUSHING
⑦
BLADE PUSHES ON POWER STROKE
KEEL
BLADE SWINGS FREE ON RETURN STROKE
SEAT
48"
18"
16" 6" 8" DECK PLAN
KEEL
30"
$\frac{1}{8}$"
HARD-PRESSED BOARD
$\frac{1}{2}$" BINDING TAPE & MARINE GLUE

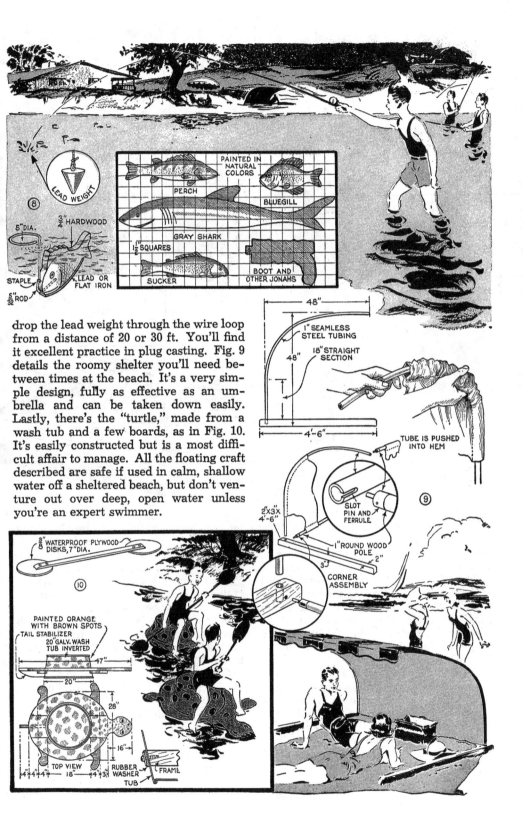

drop the lead weight through the wire loop from a distance of 20 or 30 ft. You'll find it excellent practice in plug casting. Fig. 9 details the roomy shelter you'll need between times at the beach. It's a very simple design, fully as effective as an umbrella and can be taken down easily. Lastly, there's the "turtle," made from a wash tub and a few boards, as in Fig. 10. It's easily constructed but is a most difficult affair to manage. All the floating craft described are safe if used in calm, shallow water off a sheltered beach, but don't venture out over deep, open water unless you're an expert swimmer.

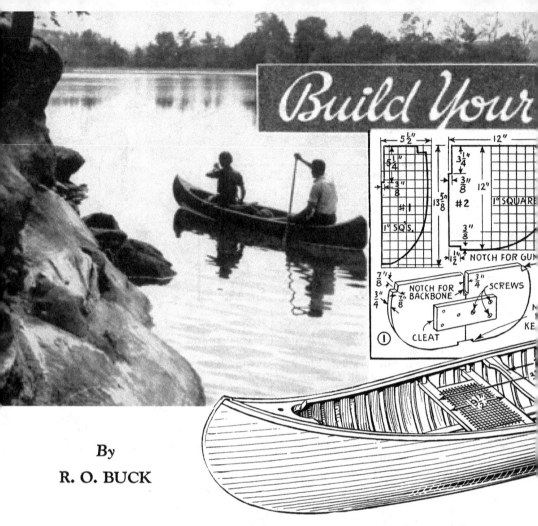

Build Your

By

R. O. BUCK

WITH its low ends and flat bottom, which extends well up into bow and stern, this 16-ft., Canadian-type canoe is well adapted to the needs of the average builder. It is used by the forestry service because of its steadiness on the water, ease of paddling and the fact that it is little affected by cross winds on account of its wide beam which is 33 in. amidships. The weight of the finished canoe will be about 70 or 80 pounds.

Construction begins with a temporary framework consisting of a set of molds and a backbone, to which the molds are fastened. Paper patterns are made from the squared drawings, Figs. 1 and 2, to trace the outline of the molds on the stock. Each mold is made in two halves, fastened together temporarily with cleats. As both ends of the canoe are identical, two molds of each size, with the exception of the cen-

ter one, are required. The backbone is a piece of ¾-in. stock 5¼ in. wide and 14 ft. 6 in. long on the upper edge and 14 ft. 4½ in. on the lower edge. See Figs. 3 and 7. The keelson is a piece of clear, straight-grained ash or oak, cut to size and tapered at each end as shown in Fig. 7.

Bending canoe stems is a cranky job, even with special equipment for the business, so you use stems built up from regular stock as in Fig. 6. The grain should run nearly at right angles as in Fig. 7, and casein glue and dowels should be used in the joint.

Assembly is started by locating and nailing the molds in position along the backbone, as in Figs. 3 and 7. The frame is then turned over and the keelson nailed temporarily to each of the molds, after which the stem pieces are screwed between the cleats at the ends of the backbone, Fig. 7.

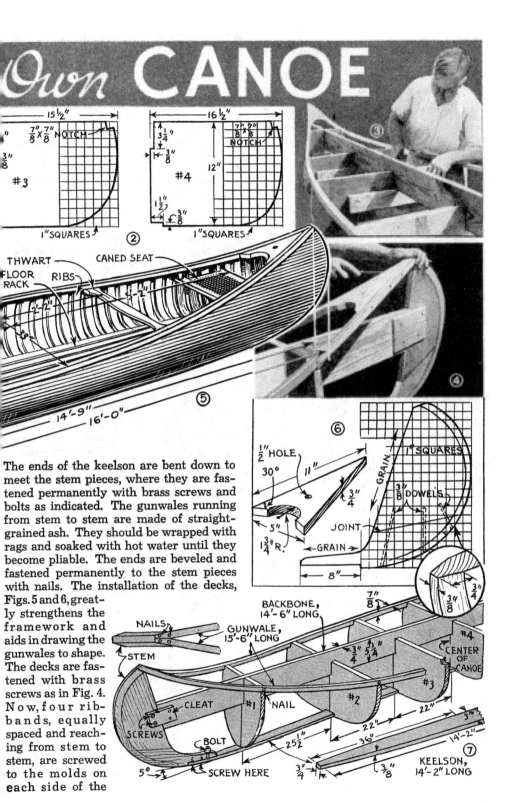

#3 — 15½" — ⅞"x⅞" NOTCH ⅜" 1"SQUARES ②

#4 — 16½" — 4¼" 1¾" ⅞" ⅞" NOTCH ⅜" 12" 1½" ⅜" 1"SQUARES

THWART — CANED SEAT — FLOOR RACK — RIBS — ③

14'-9" — 16'-0" ⑤

⑥ ½" HOLE 30° 11" ¾" GRAIN 1"SQUARES ⅜" DOWELS 5" JOINT GRAIN 1¾"R. 8"

The ends of the keelson are bent down to meet the stem pieces, where they are fastened permanently with brass screws and bolts as indicated. The gunwales running from stem to stem are made of straight-grained ash. They should be wrapped with rags and soaked with hot water until they become pliable. The ends are beveled and fastened permanently to the stem pieces with nails. The installation of the decks, Figs. 5 and 6, greatly strengthens the framework and aids in drawing the gunwales to shape. The decks are fastened with brass screws as in Fig. 4. Now, four rib-bands, equally spaced and reaching from stem to stem, are screwed to the molds on each side of the

NAILS STEM BACKBONE, 14'-6" LONG GUNWALE, 15'-6" LONG ⅞" ¾" ¾" ⅜" #4 CENTER OF CANOE #3 CLEAT #1 NAIL #2 SCREWS BOLT 22" 22" 3" 5° SCREW HERE 25½" 36" 14'-2" ¾" ⅜" KEELSON, 14'-2" LONG ⑦

saw is equipped with a ripping fence **you** will be able to save money on the ribs and planking by resawing them yourself, as shown in Fig. 10. The planks are soaked for several hours, then the first full-length plank is laid with the edge parallel with the center line of the keelson, Fig. 11, using clamps to draw it into place. Copper nails are used for fastening the planking to the ribs and all nails must be clinched across the grain on the inside of the ribs, Fig. 12. Fig. 11 shows the arrangement of the planking. Notice that the first five bilge planks run from stem to stem on each side of the keelson. The freeboard planks run out to points fore and aft as shown.

To remove the backbone, take out the cleats and saw it through at the center. Take out all but the No. 3 molds. Bolt the maple thwarts, Figs. 5 and 16, to the underside of the gunwales to prevent the hull from springing out of shape. The seat frames, Figs. 5 and 18, also may be fitted at this time. Actual measurement must determine the length of the seat stretchers. The rear stretchers are bolted direct to the keelson as shown in Figs. 8 and 9.

Although the 2-in. white-cedar ribs are $\frac{3}{16}$ in. thick instead of the usual $\frac{1}{4}$ or $\frac{5}{16}$ in., this variation does not weaken the construction as the ribs are spaced 1 in. apart to compensate. Steaming, Fig. 13, is necessary to make them sufficiently pliable to take the bends. Each rib should be long enough to reach from gunwale to gunwale over the outside of the ribbands. Begin at the center and install each rib as shown in Fig. 14, drawing it into position with C-clamps and nailing at the keelson and gunwales, starting at the center of the canoe and working toward the ends. The ribs in front of the first mold are bent so sharply that it is practically impossible to prevent them from splintering. Where a rib comes over a mold, it is simply spaced out and omitted temporarily, Fig. 15, until the molds have been removed.

When the ribs are all in place, the ribbands are taken off, making the job ready for the $\frac{1}{8}$-in. cedar planking. If your band

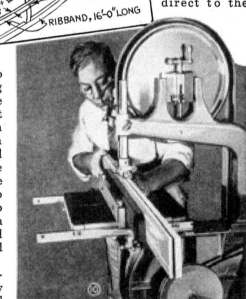

gunwales but the two forward are lowered 3 in. by means of hardwood spacers as in Fig. 18.

For canvassing you need two pieces of 8-oz. canvas, long enough to reach from stem to stem with about a foot to spare, and wide enough to reach from the gunwale to the keel with allowance for a lap. Start by spreading the canvas over half of the canoe, tacking temporarily near the center of the gunwale. Pull the covering tightly around the bilge and place a few tacks along the keel, near the center. Wet the canvas and pull it lengthwise over the stems, and tack. As it dries, the fabric will stretch and take the shape of the hull. When dry, pull out the tacks at one end and fit the canvas neatly around the stem,

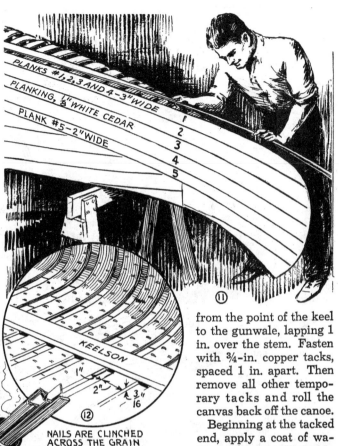

PLANKS #1,2,3 AND 4—3" WIDE

PLANKING, ⅛" WHITE CEDAR

PLANK #5—2" WIDE

1
2
3
4
5

⑪

KEELSON

1"
2"
3/16"

⑫

NAILS ARE CLINCHED ACROSS THE GRAIN

⑬

C - CLAMPS

RIBBANDS

TRIM OFF NAIL HERE ⑭ RIB

⑮

from the point of the keel to the gunwale, lapping 1 in. over the stem. Fasten with ¾-in. copper tacks, spaced 1 in. apart. Then remove all other temporary tacks and roll the canvas back off the canoe.

Beginning at the tacked end, apply a coat of waterproof canvas cement to a section of the planking along the keel, using a stiff brush, Fig. 17. Do not cover a large area as the cement dries quickly. Unroll the canvas over the cemented area, pull tightly lengthwise and fasten the loose end temporarily while tacks are placed closely along the gunwale and keel of the cemented portion. As you tack be sure that the cloth lies flat without any wrinkles. Then squeegee the canvas with the palm of the hand to make sure that it is in contact with the cement at all points. Take the next section of the hull in the same manner continuing by successive stages until you finish at the opposite stem. The second half is stretched and tacked in the same manner as the first allowing for the lap under the keel. This done, you trim the canvas along

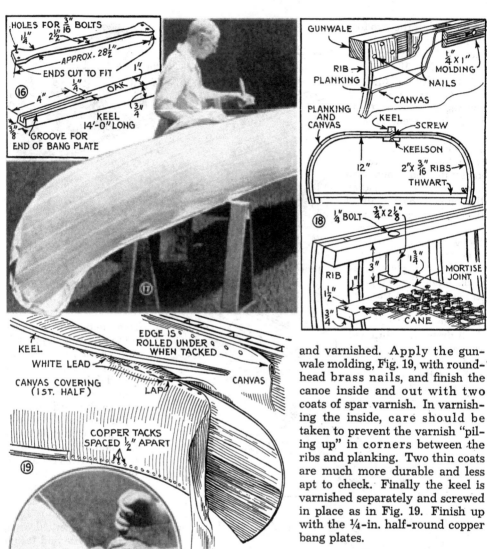

and varnished. Apply the gunwale molding, Fig. 19, with round-head brass nails, and finish the canoe inside and out with two coats of spar varnish. In varnishing the inside, care should be taken to prevent the varnish "piling up" in corners between the ribs and planking. Two thin coats are much more durable and less apt to check. Finally the keel is varnished separately and screwed in place as in Fig. 19. Finish up with the ¼-in. half-round copper bang plates.

Screws Held in Pressed Wood by Cellulose Cement

Difficulty of anchoring screws in pressed wood is overcome by filling the hole drilled to drive the screw with cellulose cement or thick lacquer. After it has

dried the screw is driven into place. Within an hour the cement will have dried to the pressed wood about the screw so that the latter is held securely.

the gunwales and finish tacking the stems, using copper tacks, which should be spaced about ½ in. apart.

Allow a few days for drying, then apply a coat of canvas cement over the entire surface. When dry, sand smooth and finish with one coat of deck paint and one of flat color after which it is again sanded

Small STEAM ENGINE
develops high speed

This one, with its rotary valve, is very simple to build and is suitable for driving model speedboats

THERE are only three parts of this steam engine that require lathe work: the flywheel, crankshaft and piston. The rest of the work is done with a file, drill and soldering iron. The sectional detail, Fig. 3, shows all parts in proper relation. Cylinder, crankshaft bearing and connecting rod are of brass, the steam pipes copper, and the other parts of steel, Fig. 2. Operating diagrams are shown in Fig. 1. The crankshaft serves as a rotary valve. On the power stroke a recess admits steam to the cylinder; at the end of the stroke the valve closes and at the beginning of the up-stroke another recess registers with the inlet tube and allows the exhaust steam to pass out through a hole drilled in the end of the craftshaft, as in Fig. 1.

Simplicity of construction is illustrated by the few parts required, Fig. 2. The crankshaft, detailed in Fig. 4, is fitted into a bushing which has been reamed ¼ in. Then the bushing is soldered to the frame, after which the piston, with wrist pin and

connecting rod assembled, is inserted into the cylinder. The latter is then soldered to the frame. A drop of solder on the crankpin will serve as a nut, although if properly fitted the connecting rod is not likely to slip off. Next, the copper steam tubes are soldered in place and a small nut is screwed on the crankshaft over the

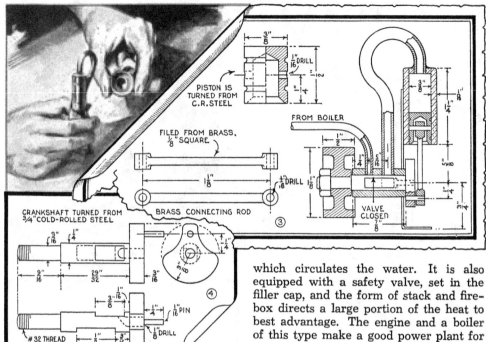

PISTON IS TURNED FROM C.R.STEEL

FILED FROM BRASS. ⅛" SQUARE

FROM BOILER

BRASS CONNECTING ROD ③

VALVE CLOSED

CRANKSHAFT TURNED FROM ¾" COLD-ROLLED STEEL

32 THREAD

④

flywheel hub make the job complete.

Detailed drawings of the crankshaft show that it must be turned down from ¾-in. cold-rolled steel, the shaft being finished to exactly ¼-in. diameter, with recesses filed away. Portions of the crank disk are removed with hacksaw and file until the proper balance with the piston and rod is attained. The crankpin must be a press fit. Dimensions of the tiny piston are given in Fig. 3. It is turned in the lathe chuck from cold-rolled steel counterbored and grooved as shown. These grooves catch and hold oil, forming an effective seal. The piston is turned to length and the hole for the wrist pin drilled. A connecting rod is filed from a piece of brass or bronze, and drilled as indicated. It should be assembled with the piston for lapping the latter to the cylinder. Chuck the cylinder in the lathe, coat the piston with polishing rouge, then slide it back and forth while the lathe is running.

Although the engine will run on compressed air, it operates better with steam. Figs. 5 to 9 detail the construction of an efficient boiler of the marine type with a coiled water tube directly over the burner,

which circulates the water. It is also equipped with a safety valve, set in the filler cap, and the form of stack and firebox directs a large portion of the heat to best advantage. The engine and a boiler of this type make a good power plant for a model speedboat.

To make the coil, a hardwood stick is trimmed down to oval section as shown in Fig. 8, and seven turns of copper tubing are wrapped around it. The coils are removed from the form and partly flattened as shown. Opposite ends of the coils are then- silver-soldered to the boiler as in Fig. 9. Note that the copper coil has one end soldered at the bottom of the boiler, the other end just below the center of the boiler head, this to promote circulation of the water. The filler cap, with the safety valve, is made of brass. Note that the flange for the filler cap is silver-soldered to the boiler shell. The important point to bear in mind is that the diameter of the valve seat must not be much over 3/16 in. unless a fairly heavy spring is used. The valve seat also serves as a filler cap. The boiler is supported in the firebox by brass angles silver-soldered to the boiler shell as in Fig. 6. With the exception of the inner side of the stack, the firebox is cut from a single sheet of galvanized iron as in Fig. 7. The joints must be riveted, as ordinary solder would melt. Small nails cut off and peened over are used for rivets. The fuel box is simply bent in shape from a single piece of galvanized iron and

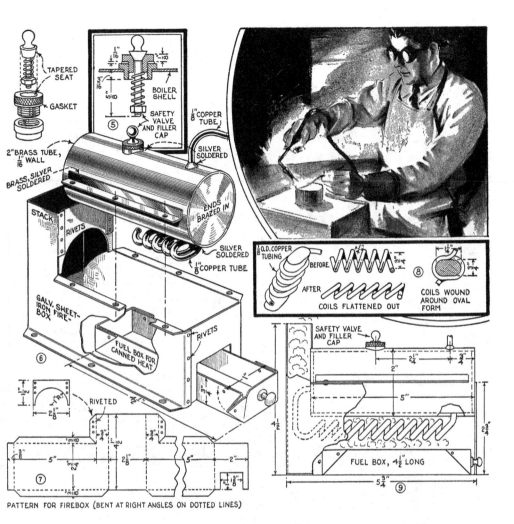

is intended for the use of "canned" fuel. To run the engine, fill the boiler three-fifths full of hot water and add a few drops of auto-engine oil. Whether mounted on a board or in a boat, both boiler and engine should be screwed down to a base.

Pedestal Bird Bath of Concrete Resembles a Tree Trunk

The home owner who wants to try his hand at making novel articles of concrete will find this bird bath a useful as well as a decorative article. Simulating a hollowed ring cut from a tree trunk and nested between four stub branches, the bath is a single concrete unit formed by applying cement to a framework of metal lath. The serrated lines imitating bark were scratched in the surface of the concrete before it hardened. The water receptable was formed over a sheet-metal disk with metal lath bound around the edges, the disk being set on top of the main framework so that the entire assembly was formed into a single unit as the cement was applied. The bath was built on a concrete platform large enough to keep it from tipping.

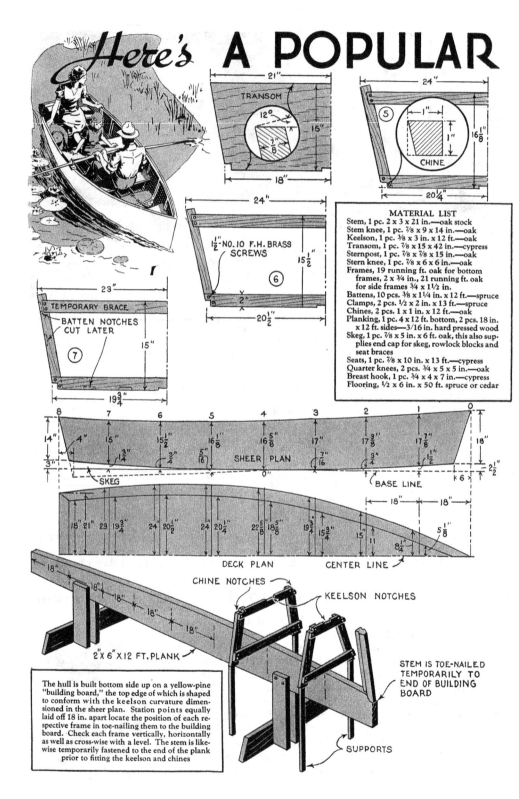

Here's A POPULAR

TRANSOM — 21" · 15" · 12° · 7/8 · 18"

CHINE — 24" · 1" · 1" · 16 1/8" · 20 1/4" · ⑤

1 1/2" NO. 10 F.H. BRASS SCREWS · 24" · 15 1/2" · 20 1/2" · 2" · ⑥

TEMPORARY BRACE · BATTEN NOTCHES CUT LATER · 23" · 15" · 19 3/4" · ⑦

MATERIAL LIST

Stem, 1 pc. 2 x 3 x 21 in.—oak stock
Stem knee, 1 pc. 7/8 x 9 x 14 in.—oak
Keelson, 1 pc. 3/8 x 3 in. x 12 ft.—oak
Transom, 1 pc. 7/8 x 15 x 42 in.—cypress
Sternpost, 1 pc. 7/8 x 7/8 x 15 in.—oak
Stern knee, 1 pc. 7/8 x 6 x 6 in.—oak
Frames, 19 running ft. oak for bottom
  frames, 2 x 3/4 in., 21 running ft. oak
  for side frames 3/4 x 1 1/2 in.
Battens, 10 pcs. 3/8 x 1 1/4 in. x 12 ft.—spruce
Clamps, 2 pcs. 1/2 x 2 in. x 13 ft.—spruce
Chines, 2 pcs. 1 x 1 in. x 12 ft.—oak
Planking, 1 pc. 4 x 12 ft. bottom, 2 pcs. 18 in.
  x 12 ft. sides—3/16 in. hard pressed wood
Skeg, 1 pc. 7/8 x 5 in. x 6 ft. oak, this also sup-
  plies end cap for skeg, rowlock blocks and
  seat braces
Seats, 1 pc. 7/8 x 10 in. x 13 ft.—cypress
Quarter knees, 2 pcs. 3/4 x 5 x 5 in.—oak
Breast hook, 1 pc. 3/4 x 4 x 7 in.—cypress
Flooring, 1/2 x 6 in. x 50 ft. spruce or cedar

SHEER PLAN · BASE LINE · SKEG · 14" · 3" · 18" · 2 1/2"

DECK PLAN · CENTER LINE · CHINE NOTCHES · KEELSON NOTCHES

2" x 6" x 12 FT. PLANK · SUPPORTS

STEM IS TOE-NAILED TEMPORARILY TO END OF BUILDING BOARD

The hull is built bottom side up on a yellow-pine "building board," the top edge of which is shaped to conform with the keelson curvature dimensioned in the sheer plan. Station points equally laid off 18 in. apart locate the position of each respective frame in toe-nailing them to the building board. Check each frame vertically, horizontally as well as cross-wise with a level. The stem is likewise temporarily fastened to the end of the plank prior to fitting the keelson and chines

Twelve-Foot ROW BOAT

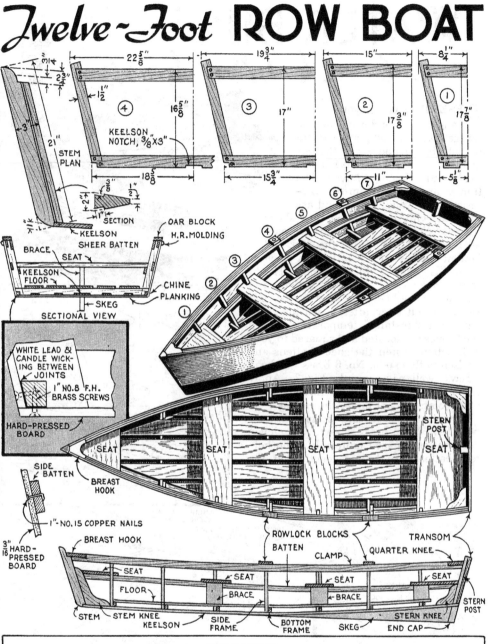

STEM PLAN

KEELSON NOTCH, 3/8 X 3"

④ 22 5/8" 16 5/8" 1 1/2" 3 1/4" 2 3/4" 21" 3" 18 5/8" 3/4" 1/2" 2" 1"

③ 19 3/4" 17" 15 3/4"

② 15" 17 3/8" 11"

① 8 1/4" 17 7/8" 5 1/8"

SECTION

OAR BLOCK
H.R. MOLDING

KEELSON
SHEER BATTEN
BRACE
SEAT
KEELSON
FLOOR
SKEG
CHINE
PLANKING
SECTIONAL VIEW

WHITE LEAD &
CANDLE WICK-
ING BETWEEN
JOINTS
1" NO.8 F.H.
BRASS SCREWS
HARD-PRESSED
BOARD

SIDE
BATTEN
BREAST
HOOK
1"-NO.15 COPPER NAILS
3/16" HARD-
PRESSED
BOARD

BREAST HOOK
STEM
STEM KNEE
KEELSON
SEAT
FLOOR
SIDE
FRAME
BRACE
BOTTOM
FRAME
SKEG
SEAT
ROWLOCK BLOCKS
BATTEN
CLAMP
BRACE
STERN KNEE
END CAP
SEAT
TRANSOM
QUARTER KNEE
STERN
POST

STERN
POST
SEAT

PROCEDURE

1. Construct "building board" trestle from 12-ft. plank as shown.
2. Cut the seven frames to size and assemble with F. H. brass screws.
3. Center the frames and nail them upright to the "building board."
4. Cut the stem to shape from 2-in. oak and fasten to the plank end.
5. Fasten keelson and chines in place with 1½-in. No. 10 F. H. brass screws and plane chines down flush with side frames.
6. Cut batten notches 3/8 in. deep in transom and side and bottom frames and fasten battens with 1¼-in. No. 6 F. H. brass screws
7. Shape and fit the breast hook and the stem and the stern knees next.
8. Lay candle wicking in white lead along the chines and transom, and cover the sides of hull first with single panels of 3/16-in. hard pressed board, fastening to frames, stem, chines and transom with 1-in. brass screws spaced 1 in. Cover bottom in same manner.
9. Fit clamp boards and quarter knees at stern and then add floor boards, seat risers and seats. Cover stem with 1-in. iron nosing.

"WATER BUG"
a beach play boat

RESEMBLING a kayak in both appearance and construction, this canvas-covered play boat can be built by anyone—even the beginner in boatbuilding. It handles easily and will not tip over. The frames are cut from moisture-resisting plywood, Fig. 1, and assembled with the keelson and sheer battens. Note that the battens are parallel as in Fig. 4, and that the deck and bottom curves are identical in each frame as well as the transom. The frames are spaced in their relative positions along the keelson with nails that can be drawn out later, after which the sheer battens are installed temporarily. When the frames are located and squared to your satisfaction, fasten the sheer battens and keelson with 1¼-in. No. 6 brass flat-head screws, well countersunk, Fig. 2. Apply casein waterproof glue to these and all other joints, except under the canvas.

Now install deck and bottom battens with 1-in. No. 6 brass screws. Use eleven deck battens spaced uniformly. The bottom battens are butted together at the

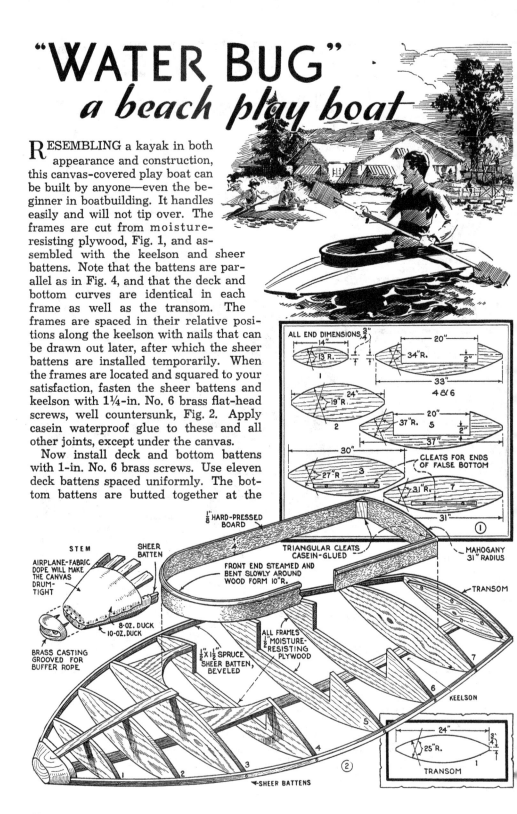

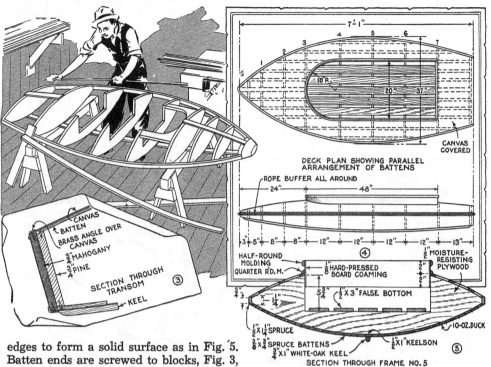

DECK PLAN SHOWING PARALLEL
ARRANGEMENT OF BATTENS

ROPE BUFFER ALL AROUND

CANVAS
COVERED

HALF-ROUND
MOLDING
QUARTER RD.M.

1" HARD-PRESSED
8 BOARD COAMING

1/2" MOISTURE-
RESISTING
PLYWOOD

CANVAS
BATTEN
BRASS ANGLE OVER
CANVAS
3/4"MAHOGANY
3/8"PINE

SECTION THROUGH
TRANSOM ③

KEEL

5¾" ½"X 3"FALSE BOTTOM

10-OZ.DUCK

1½"X 1½"SPRUCE
3/8"X ¾"SPRUCE BATTENS
¾"X 1" WHITE-OAK KEEL

½"X1"KEELSON ⑤

SECTION THROUGH FRAME NO. 5

edges to form a solid surface as in Fig. 5. Batten ends are screwed to blocks, Fig. 3, so that they are flush with surfaces of stem and transom. This permits the canvas to be stretched smoothly. Before fitting the cockpit coaming, lay the bottom canvas (10-oz. duck), stretching it snugly all around and tacking along the top of the sheer battens and over the stem piece. It is also tacked over the edge of the transom. Apply marine glue along the edges of the wood, and stagger copper tacks about ½ in. apart. The tacks are covered with a brass strip or angle, which is screwed down.

Trim away the canvas around the edge and put the deck canvas on. This laps over the sheer battens to which it is tacked after marine glue has been applied under it. Tack around the edges of the cockpit, using marine glue as before. Next, apply airplane fabric dope to deck and bottom canvas. When this is thoroughly dry the cockpit opening in the canvas can be cut out with a razor blade and the coaming fitted in place. The coaming, by the way, is a single strip of ⅛-in. hard-pressed board, which has been steamed and bent to a semicircle around a wood frame. The back of the cockpit is fitted with mahogany. Molding around the top of the coam-

ing stiffens and protects the edge, and gives a finished effect.

A false bottom can be made fixed, or removable. Around the sheer battens, over the tacks, screw a hardwood strip about ¾ by ¼ in., and to this secure a rope buffer all the way around, and through the groove in the brass nosepiece. If desired, weight of the boat can be reduced considerably by sawing out some of the central area of the plywood frames; even ¼ instead of ⅜-in. battens are permissible. And to render the craft non-sinkable in case the canvas is punctured, an inflated inner tube can be put under fore and after decks. The doped canvas can be made smooth and slick by several alternate applications of paint and fine sandpaper, finishing with two coats of spar varnish.

Filling Cracks at Baseboards

If baseboards or wall molding have pulled away from a wall and cannot be renailed, fill the crack with paste wood filler mixed to the consistency of soft putty. Push it into the crack and then run the finger over the filler several times to make it smooth.

FUN *with these* BATHERS' FLOATS

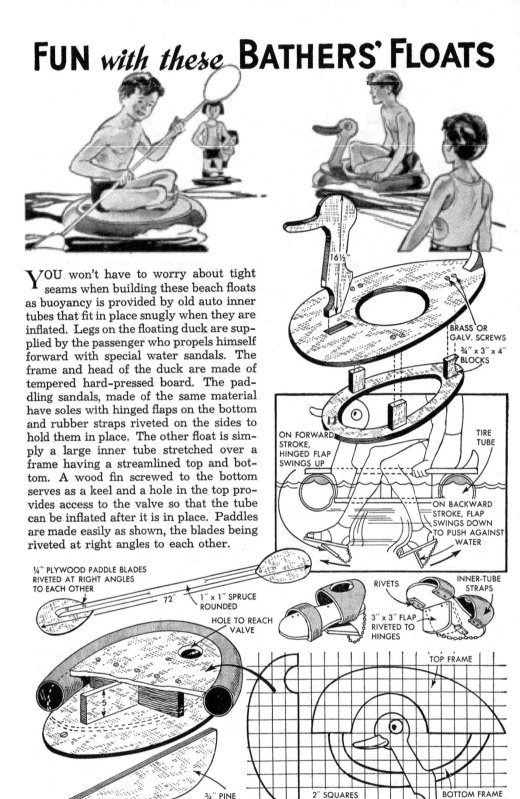

YOU won't have to worry about tight seams when building these beach floats as buoyancy is provided by old auto inner tubes that fit in place snugly when they are inflated. Legs on the floating duck are supplied by the passenger who propels himself forward with special water sandals. The frame and head of the duck are made of tempered hard-pressed board. The paddling sandals, made of the same material have soles with hinged flaps on the bottom and rubber straps riveted on the sides to hold them in place. The other float is simply a large inner tube stretched over a frame having a streamlined top and bottom. A wood fin screwed to the bottom serves as a keel and a hole in the top provides access to the valve so that the tube can be inflated after it is in place. Paddles are made easily as shown, the blades being riveted at right angles to each other.

16½"

BRASS OR GALV. SCREWS

¾" x 3" x 4" BLOCKS

TIRE TUBE

ON FORWARD STROKE, HINGED FLAP SWINGS UP

ON BACKWARD STROKE, FLAP SWINGS DOWN TO PUSH AGAINST WATER

¼" PLYWOOD PADDLE BLADES RIVETED AT RIGHT ANGLES TO EACH OTHER

72"

1" x 1" SPRUCE ROUNDED

HOLE TO REACH VALVE

RIVETS

INNER-TUBE STRAPS

3" x 3" FLAP RIVETED TO HINGES

5"

¾" PINE KEEL

TOP FRAME

2" SQUARES

BOTTOM FRAME

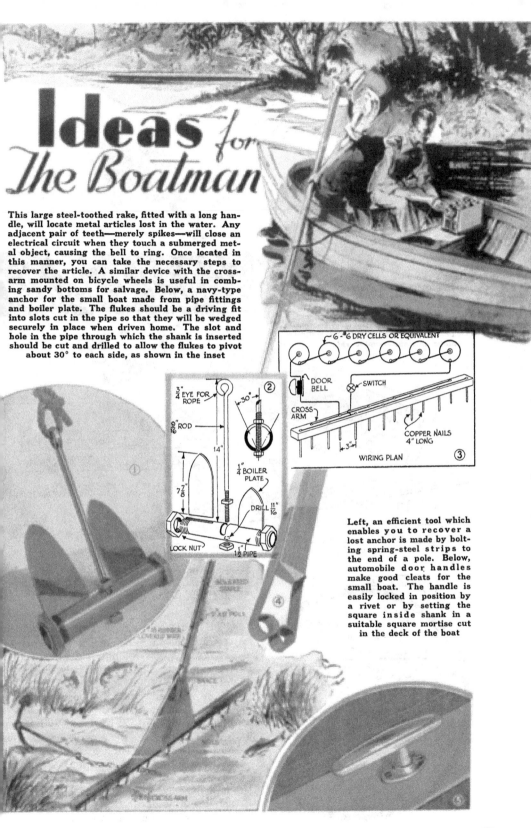

Ideas for The Boatman

This large steel-toothed rake, fitted with a long handle, will locate metal articles lost in the water. Any adjacent pair of teeth—merely spikes—will close an electrical circuit when they touch a submerged metal object, causing the bell to ring. Once located in this manner, you can take the necessary steps to recover the article. A similar device with the cross-arm mounted on bicycle wheels is useful in combing sandy bottoms for salvage. Below, a navy-type anchor for the small boat made from pipe fittings and boiler plate. The flukes should be a driving fit into slots cut in the pipe so that they will be wedged securely in place when driven home. The slot and hole in the pipe through which the shank is inserted should be cut and drilled to allow the flukes to pivot about 30° to each side, as shown in the inset

6 - №6 DRY CELLS OR EQUIVALENT

DOOR BELL
SWITCH
CROSS ARM
COPPER NAILS 4" LONG
WIRING PLAN ③

¾" EYE FOR ROPE
-30°-
³⁄₁₆" ROD
14"
¼" BOILER PLATE
7⅞"
DRILL ¹¹⁄₁₆"
LOCK NUT
1½ PIPE
②

Left, an efficient tool which enables you to recover a lost anchor is made by bolting spring-steel strips to the end of a pole. Below, automobile door handles make good cleats for the small boat. The handle is easily locked in position by a rivet or by setting the square inside shank in a suitable square mortise cut in the deck of the boat

67

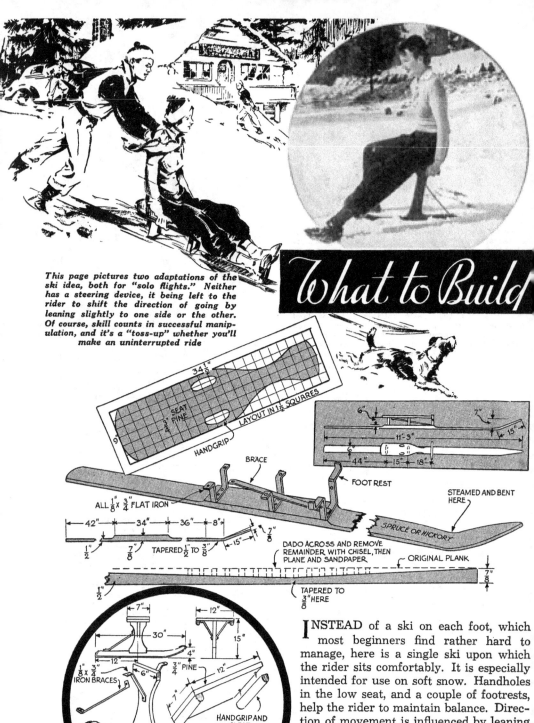

This page pictures two adaptations of the ski idea, both for "solo flights." Neither has a steering device, it being left to the rider to shift the direction of going by leaning slightly to one side or the other. Of course, skill counts in successful manipulation, and it's a "toss-up" whether you'll make an uninterrupted ride

What to Build

SEAT PINE
LAYOUT IN 1½ SQUARES
HANDGRIP
BRACE
FOOT REST
STEAMED AND BENT HERE
ALL ⅛" X ¾" FLAT IRON
SPRUCE OR HICKORY
TAPERED ½" TO ⅜"
DADO ACROSS AND REMOVE REMAINDER WITH CHISEL, THEN PLANE AND SANDPAPER
ORIGINAL PLANK
TAPERED TO ⅜" HERE
IRON BRACES
PINE
HANDGRIP AND CLEAT
COUNTERSUNK SCREWS
5" X ¼" DEEP
1/16" X ⅝" IRON SHOE

INSTEAD of a ski on each foot, which most beginners find rather hard to manage, here is a single ski upon which the rider sits comfortably. It is especially intended for use on soft snow. Handholes in the low seat, and a couple of footrests, help the rider to maintain balance. Direction of movement is influenced by leaning toward either side. A variation of this idea is the single-runner scooter, shown in the two circles. The runner is short and has an iron shoe, for use on hard-packed snow or ice. The high seat, which has handgrips underneath, requires greater dexterity in balancing this than the ski.

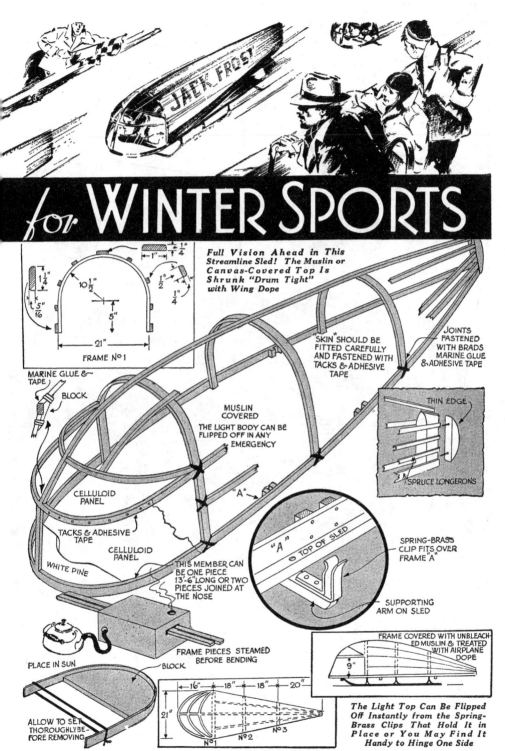

for WINTER SPORTS

Full Vision Ahead in This Streamline Sled! The Muslin or Canvas-Covered Top Is Shrunk "Drum Tight" with Wing Dope

1"
1¼"
1"
¼"
10½"
1¼"
1½"
1¼"
5⁄16"
5"
21"

FRAME N°1

MARINE GLUE & TAPE

BLOCK

"SKIN" SHOULD BE FITTED CAREFULLY AND FASTENED WITH TACKS & ADHESIVE TAPE

JOINTS FASTENED WITH BRADS MARINE GLUE & ADHESIVE TAPE

MUSLIN COVERED

THE LIGHT BODY CAN BE FLIPPED OFF IN ANY EMERGENCY

THIN EDGE

SPRUCE LONGERONS

CELLULOID PANEL

TACKS & ADHESIVE TAPE

CELLULOID PANEL

WHITE PINE

"A"

"A" TOP OF SLED

SPRING-BRASS CLIP FITS OVER FRAME "A"

SUPPORTING ARM ON SLED

THIS MEMBER CAN BE ONE PIECE 13'-6" LONG OR TWO PIECES JOINED AT THE NOSE

PLACE IN SUN

FRAME PIECES STEAMED BEFORE BENDING

BLOCK

ALLOW TO SET THOROUGHLY BEFORE REMOVING

16" 18" 18" 20"

21"

N°1 N°2 N°3

FRAME COVERED WITH UNBLEACHED MUSLIN & TREATED WITH AIRPLANE DOPE

9"

The Light Top Can Be Flipped Off Instantly from the Spring-Brass Clips That Hold It in Place or You May Find It Handy to Hinge One Side

This "bi-skee" is especially designed for use as a winter coasting bicycle. It is made of white pine with the exception of bearing brackets, hinges and a few fittings. Dowels and plywood gussets reinforce all joints, waterproof casein glue being used wherever possible. The brake pedal takes the place of the usual bicycle foot crank.

The toboggan appears much like the conventional design, but it is narrower

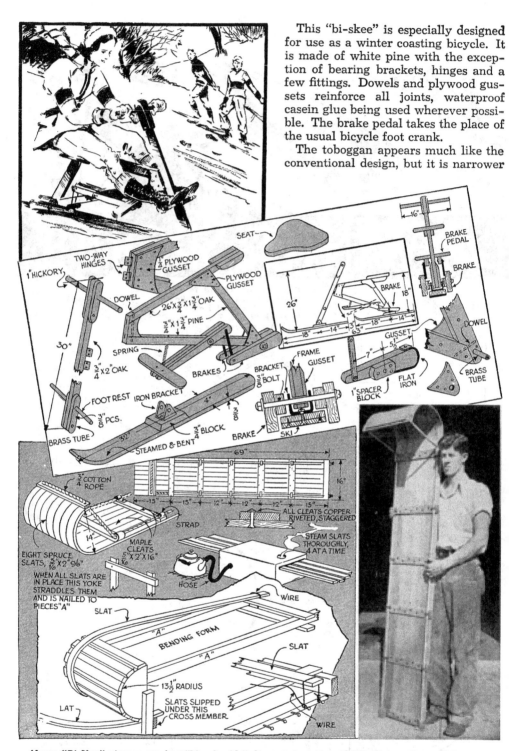

Above, "Bi-Skee" gives you a fast "bicycle ride" down a snow-covered hill. Too much speed, however, may call for the application of brakes that are foot-controlled. Below, for most purposes of tobogganing, this 6-ft. job will be just the thing. The curved front is uniformly bent on the form shown

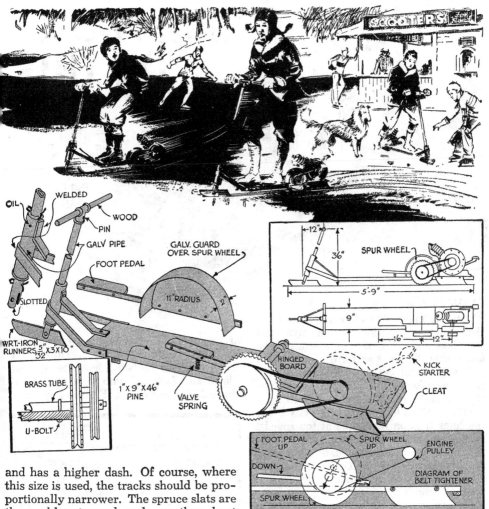

and has a higher dash. Of course, where this size is used, the tracks should be proportionally narrower. The spruce slats are thoroughly steamed and are then bent over the form, being held down at the other end with wire. When the slats have all been bent, they are straddled with a yoke so they will lie flat. After drying for 48 hrs. in dry weather, the slats are removed and assembled to maple cleats by copper-riveting. When the job is finished apply several coats of shellac, rubbing each with steel wool when dry. The finish coat is sandpapered and waxed.

The motor-driven scooter has wrought-iron runners, a single one at the front which is used for steering, and two at the rear. The spur wheel is covered with a guard and is driven by the belt only when the foot pedal is depressed. Motor-control lines should be handy on the steering bar and a foot brake should be provided.

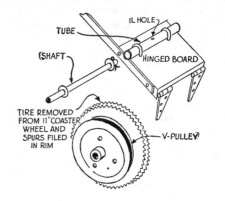

Motor-Driven Scooter Is the Outstanding Number in the Winter Ice Carnival; You Can Obtain Small Gas Engines for This Purpose

Express Ride
ON THIS

20"

16"

FRONT VIEW
①

SAFETY features are built right into the streamline design of this speedy bobsled. The steering cables are always taut; feet, legs and arms of the passengers are lower than the seat and are protected by a heavy metal-faced guard which also serves as a footrest; a box-type body gives rigidity and strength combined with light weight, while a low center of gravity holds the liner true on its course at top speeds. Although this is a six-passenger job, it can be made to accommodate eight passengers, or cut back for only four persons without altering any dimensions save the over-all length.

General details are given in Figs. 1, 2 and 3. Assembly of the body is shown in Fig. 3, along with a sectional view of the box construction. Use brass or galvanized screws, with the heads countersunk, and waterproof casein glue in all joints. The bulkheads are of ⅞-in. pine. Side members are of ¾-in. pine with handholds spaced at 12-in. intervals as shown. To these are screwed the footrests, made up of individual pieces to simplify sawing. The strap-iron guard rail is screwed along the outside. For the steering assembly mount a steering wheel from a model-T Ford on a steel shaft. On the lower end, to increase the diameter only, fit a short section of pipe with a cap on the lower end. An eyebolt without nut is screwed into this and the shaft. This eyebolt also serves to keep the cable from slipping. A section

of brass tube is installed in the upright block for a bearing as in Fig. 3. The curved wood brace is rabbeted into the upright block, and fastened with long screws up through the seat board. For the bumper a

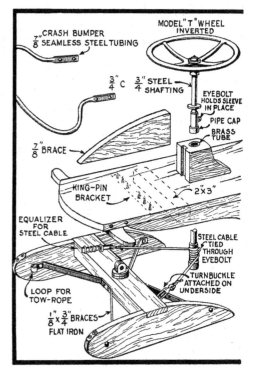

MODEL "T" WHEEL INVERTED

CRASH BUMPER
⅞" SEAMLESS STEEL TUBING

¾" C ¾" STEEL SHAFTING

EYEBOLT HOLDS SLEEVE IN PLACE

PIPE CAP

BRASS TUBE

⅞" BRACE

KING-PIN BRACKET

2"x3"

EQUALIZER FOR STEEL CABLE

STEEL CABLE TIED THROUGH EYEBOLT

TURNBUCKLE ATTACHED ON UNDERSIDE

LOOP FOR TOW-ROPE

⅛"x¾" BRACES FLAT IRON

STURDY "SNOWLINER"

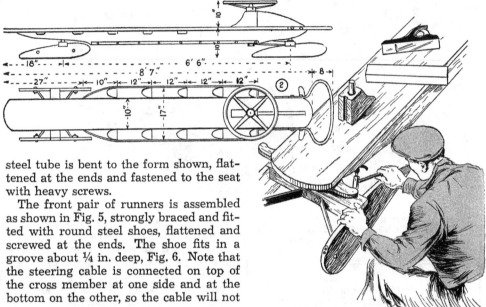

steel tube is bent to the form shown, flattened at the ends and fastened to the seat with heavy screws.

The front pair of runners is assembled as shown in Fig. 5, strongly braced and fitted with round steel shoes, flattened and screwed at the ends. The shoe fits in a groove about ¼ in. deep, Fig. 6. Note that the steering cable is connected on top of the cross member at one side and at the bottom on the other, so the cable will not

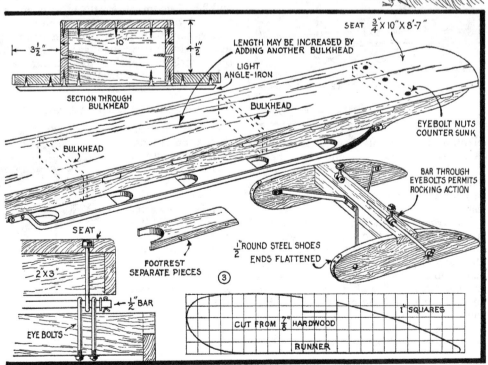

SECTION THROUGH BULKHEAD

LENGTH MAY BE INCREASED BY ADDING ANOTHER BULKHEAD

LIGHT ANGLE-IRON

BULKHEAD

BULKHEAD

SEAT ¾" X 10" X 8'-7"

EYEBOLT NUTS COUNTER SUNK

BAR THROUGH EYEBOLTS PERMITS ROCKING ACTION

SEAT

FOOTREST SEPARATE PIECES

½" ROUND STEEL SHOES ENDS FLATTENED

2"X3"

½" BAR

EYE BOLTS

CUT FROM ⅞" HARDWOOD

RUNNER

1" SQUARES

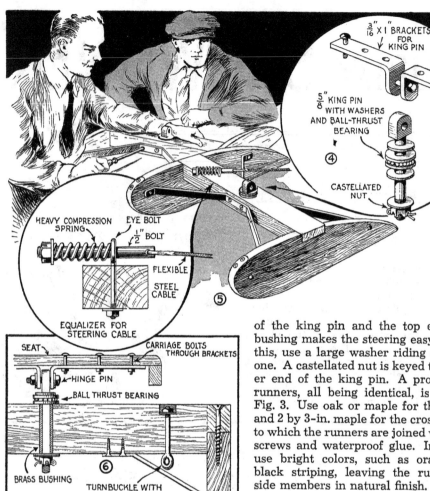

of the king pin and the top end of the bushing makes the steering easy. Lacking this, use a large washer riding on a brass one. A castellated nut is keyed to the lower end of the king pin. A profile of the runners, all being identical, is shown in Fig. 3. Use oak or maple for the runners and 2 by 3-in. maple for the cross member, to which the runners are joined with heavy screws and waterproof glue. In painting, use bright colors, such as orange, with black striping, leaving the runners and side members in natural finish.

Drills Held in Can of Lead Shot

Filled with small shot, a can or glass makes a good holder for your twist drills. This holder is heavy and is not easily upset, and a little oil dropped on the shot will help keep the drills from rusting. The can of shot also has an advantage over the usual type of holder in that the drills can be inserted anywhere without stopping your work to insert them carefully in holes.

climb on the steering shaft. A turnbuckle is inserted at one end, and the other is connected with an equalizing coil spring, so that the cable will be under tension in any position. Use a ³⁄₁₆-in. woven-steel cable.

The front runners oscillate by means of a bracket made of two angles and attached to the bottom of the seat. A bolt through the two halves of the bracket and the flattened top of the king pin forms the pivot, as in Figs. 4 and 6. The king pin can be made by flattening the head of a ⅝-in. machine bolt, then drilling for a ½-in. hinge pin. The king pin turns in a brass bushing, Fig. 6. A ball thrust bearing between the head

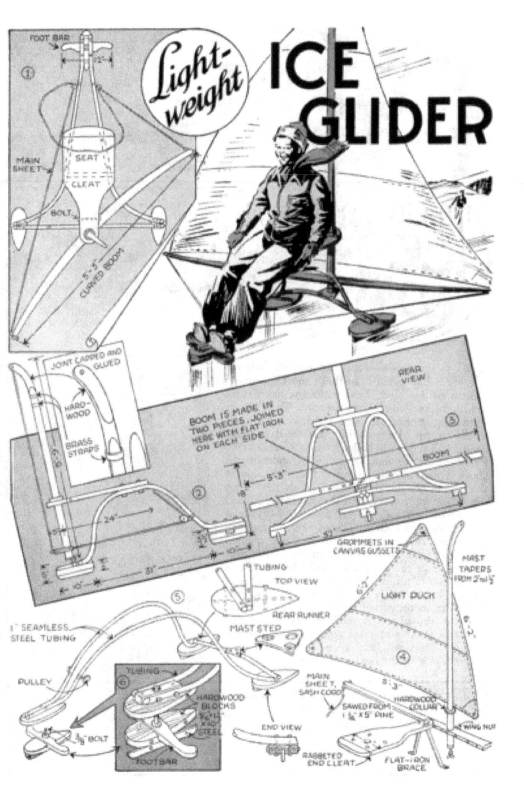

Light-weight

ICE GLIDER

FOOT BAR

① 7"

MAIN SHEET

SEAT CLEAT

BOLT

5'-3" CURVED BOOM

JOINT CAPPED AND GLUED

HARD-WOOD

BRASS STRAPS

REAR VIEW

BOOM IS MADE IN TWO PIECES, JOINED HERE WITH FLAT IRON ON EACH SIDE

⑤

BOOM

5'-3"

8"

②

24"

51"

10"

GROMMETS IN CANVAS GUSSETS

MAST TAPERS FROM 2" TO 1½"

TUBING

TOP VIEW

⑤

REAR RUNNER

MAST STEP

LIGHT DUCK

6'-2"

6'-2"

1" SEAMLESS STEEL TUBING

PULLEY

TUBING

⑥

HARDWOOD BLOCKS

⅜" BOLT

FOOT BAR

MAIN SHEET, SASH CORD

SAWED FROM 1⅝" X 5" PINE

HARDWOOD COLLAR

WING NUT

END VIEW

RABBETED END CLEAT

FLAT-IRON BRACE

④

5'-3"

Model ICE BOAT

SAIL it as a model—let it tow you on skates—ride it like a big 'un—that's the three-purpose model ice boat. First make the main runner, then the two smaller runners. The bottom of the big runner can be capped with a length of flat or round metal, but the small runners need a sharp edge in order to prevent side drift. For this purpose you can use ⅛-in. sheet-metal shoes riveted into a slot cut in the underside of the runner, as shown in Fig. 1. Make the cross arm about 26 in. long, and slot it near each end to provide an adjustment for the 5-lb. lead weights used as ballast. These are not necessary when you ride the sled, but they are needed when the boat sails alone to prevent "hiking." The weights can be made easily by cutting a section out of a block of wood and using this as a mold, as shown in Fig. 2. The actual size of the boat can be varied up or down to suit. Do not try to crowd on too much sail; 10 or 12 sq. ft. is sufficient. If you want more canvas, use the gaff rig. This will add 4 or 5 ft. to the area without raising the center of effort.

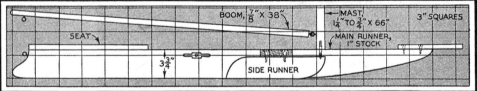

New actors on GARDEN WINDMILLS

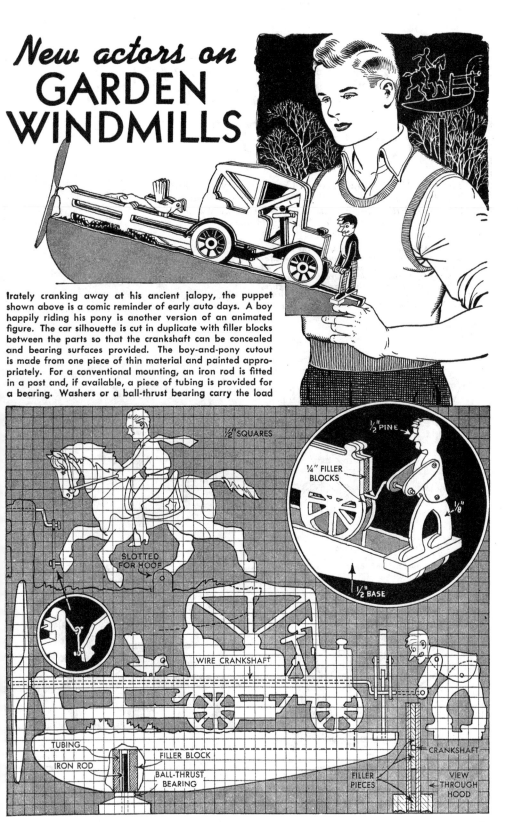

Irately cranking away at his ancient jalopy, the puppet shown above is a comic reminder of early auto days. A boy happily riding his pony is another version of an animated figure. The car silhouette is cut in duplicate with filler blocks between the parts so that the crankshaft can be concealed and bearing surfaces provided. The boy-and-pony cutout is made from one piece of thin material and painted appropriately. For a conventional mounting, an iron rod is fitted in a post and, if available, a piece of tubing is provided for a bearing. Washers or a ball-thrust bearing carry the load

½" SQUARES

½" PINE

¼" FILLER BLOCKS

⅛"

½" BASE

SLOTTED FOR HOOF

WIRE CRANKSHAFT

TUBING
FILLER BLOCK
IRON ROD
BALL-THRUST BEARING

CRANKSHAFT

FILLER PIECES

VIEW THROUGH HOOD

WHITHER BLOWS THE WIND?

The Iron Weathervane, Like Its Contemporary, the Brass Knocker, is Returning to Popularity, and an Attractive Design is Within the Means of the Average Family, as it Can be Made Mostly at Home

Black Sheet Iron Is Generally Used for Making Weathervane Silhouettes although Other Materials, Such as Duralumin and Brass, Painted Black When Finished, Are Also Suitable; the Thickness Depends on the Size of the Figure, 1/16 In. Being the Minimum; Action, with a Touch of Caricature, Has a Universal Appeal

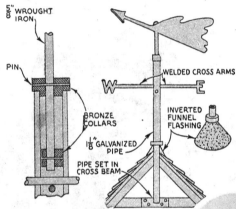

Details Showing Method of Mounting; Two Cross Arms, Indicating East and West, May Be Attached to the Support; Roof Leaks Are Avoided by Use of Flashing

Here Are Two Lively Silhouettes That You Can Enlarge on a Sheet of Paper and Transfer to the Metal; Hobbies as Well as Professions Can Be Represented

78

Electrical Indicator Blinks
WIND SPEED *and* DIRECTION

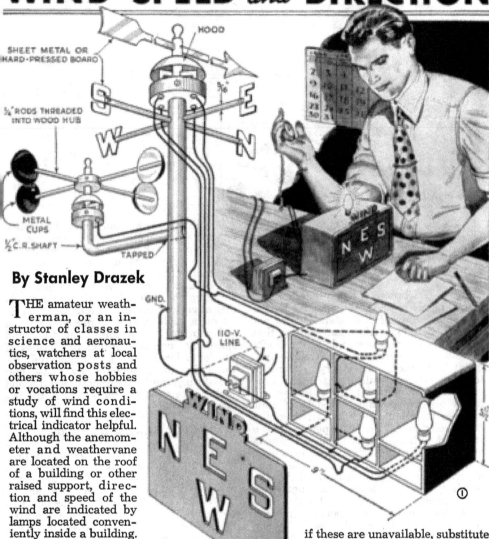

SHEET METAL OR HARD-PRESSED BOARD

HOOD

¾" RODS THREADED INTO WOOD HUB

METAL CUPS

½" C.R. SHAFT

TAPPED

GND.

110-V. LINE

WIND

N E S W

①

By Stanley Drazek

THE amateur weatherman, or an instructor of classes in science and aeronautics, watchers at local observation posts and others whose hobbies or vocations require a study of wind conditions, will find this electrical indicator helpful. Although the anemometer and weathervane are located on the roof of a building or other raised support, direction and speed of the wind are indicated by lamps located conveniently inside a building. Speed of the wind is determined by counting the flashes of a blinking lamp, and the wind direction is indicated on a panel in which the letters N, E, S and W are jigsawed. A lamp behind each letter lights up whenever the weathervane, which acts as a switch to close the electrical circuit, points in the direction designated by one of the letters.

Although construction of the indicator may seem difficult at first glance, it is quite easy. Naturally, steel shafting is best for the main standard and the arm supporting the anemometer, and brass or copper is best for the rest of the exposed parts, but

if these are unavailable, substitute materials can be used. For example, the weathervane and letters designating the directions can be tempered hard-pressed board, and the small rods supporting the letters and also the anemometer cups can be hardwood dowels. Also, it is possible to use wood for the standard and arm. If this is done, short shafts must be inserted in their upper ends to provide bearings. And, of course, the short rotating shafts of the vane and anemometer must be metal to withstand wear. If regular spun-metal wind cups for the anemometer are unavailable, the bowl parts of large spoons will serve, but they all must be of the same size and shape.

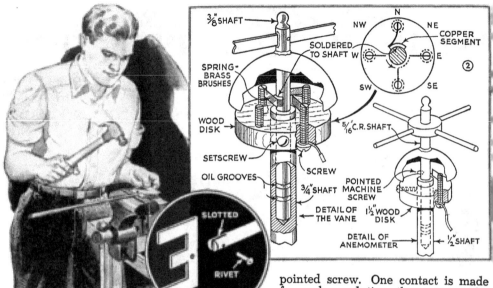

Detail of anemometer diagram labels: 3/8" SHAFT, SOLDERED TO SHAFT, SPRING-BRASS BRUSHES, WOOD DISK, SETSCREW, OIL GROOVES, 3/4" SHAFT, SCREW, DETAIL OF THE VANE, N, NW, NE, W, E, SW, SE, COPPER SEGMENT, 5/16" C.R. SHAFT, POINTED MACHINE SCREW, 1 1/2" WOOD DISK, DETAIL OF ANEMOMETER, 1/2" SHAFT

SLOTTED, RIVET

Fig. 2 shows how the pointed shafts of the anemometer and weathervane work in the drilled ends of their standards to reduce friction to a minimum. Notice that grooves near the lower ends of the shafts serve as oil reservoirs, which make frequent lubrication unnecessary. Reference to the left-hand detail of Fig. 2 will show you how to construct the weathervane brush assembly, which consists of four brushes mounted on a wooden disk, the latter being locked on the upper end of the standard with a setscrew to permit adjustment. The brushes are strips of spring brass or copper clamped in the slotted ends of screws turned up through the disk. The brushes make contact with a single-segment commutator sweat-soldered to the vane shaft. It is very important that the segment width be equal exactly to one quarter of the vane-shaft circumference, and that the segment center be exactly in line with the vane. In this way, when the indicator is wired as in Fig. 1, only one lamp will show on the indicator panel when the vane points north, east, west or south, as the commutator contacts only one brush. But, if the vane points between two of these directions, the brush will contact two adjacent brushes and two lamps will show. For example, a northeast wind would cause the north and east lamps to show. A sheet-metal hood protects the brush assembly.

Construction of the anemometer mounting and brush assembly are similar to that for the vane, except that only one brush is used, and the commutator consists of a pointed screw. One contact is made for each revolution, thus causing the lamp to flash once for each revolution. The easiest way of calibrating the anemometer is to fasten it above the front of a car and drive on a calm day, counting the revolutions of the anemometer at various speeds. This data is recorded on a scale, which is placed near the indicator to aid in computing the wind speed by anyone counting the flashes of the lamp for 1 min. Electric current for the indicator is supplied by a 6-8-volt transformer, and Christmas-tree bulbs and sockets are used for the lamps at the indicating panel.

Handy Dispenser From Fruit Jar

Where small, measured amounts of materials, such as tea, coffee, soap flakes, etc., are to be poured from containers, this easy-to-make dispenser will come in handy, as all you have to do is tip it upside down to pour out the predetermined amount. A fruit jar is used and the lid is fitted with a tube as shown, the lower end of which is provided with a concave or cupped piece of tin of a size to hold the desired amount of material to be dispensed.

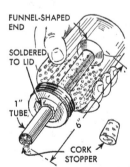

FUNNEL-SHAPED END, SOLDERED TO LID, 1" TUBE, CORK STOPPER

When the dispenser contains a material from which air should be excluded, a cork can be inserted in the end of the tube and a rubber can be used under the jar lid.

Electricity Plays This One-String 'Vibro' Fiddle

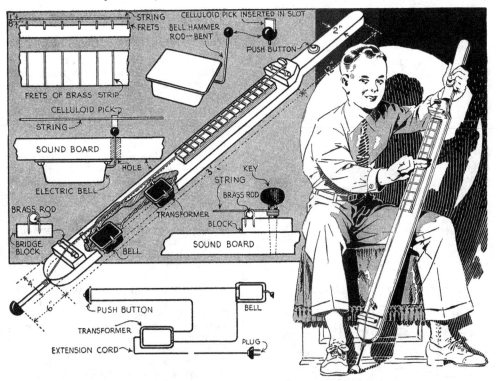

Here's a one-stringed musical instrument that can be played wherever 110-volt current is available. Principal parts required are a sounding board, a steel guitar string, a doorbell and transformer with push-button switch and a few odds and ends of brass and steel rod. The sounding board is a length of ¾-in. pine, 48 in. long and 4 in. wide. One end is tapered for a comfortable handhold, the other rounded as shown. A hole in the lower end of the board takes a 6-in. length of steel rod, one end of which is fitted with a rubber chair tip. Blocks of softwood form a bridge for the string, which is tensioned with a key taken from an old banjo or guitar, and fitted into a tapered hole in the upper block. The fret board is of thin wood grooved at right angles for strips of sheet brass all cut to exactly the same width. These are placed at distances to give the proper pitched notes of the scale. Some experimentation will be necessary due to variations in the sounding board. The ball of the striker is slotted to take a celluloid pick as shown. The switch controls this action nicely. Holding down the push button slurs the notes, while releasing it between notes gives a staccato effect.

Paper Cone Holds Bottle Cap to Serve Hot Coffee

When hot coffee is carried in an insulated bottle, and no extra cup or container is at hand in which to serve it, a piece of paper from the lunch basket may be rolled to form a cone into which the bottle cap will fit quite snugly. With this holder, which keeps it from burning the hand, the cap will provide a convenient and comfortable cup for the purpose.

SIX-VOLT BLINKER and CODE

By Arthur I. Rattray

A DAPTABLE to all code-practice applications, this unusually simple combination unit requires a minimum of parts and provides the radio student with a practical means of learning code by either the visual or audible method. Both systems can be operated by the same key either simultaneously or individually.

The oscillator tube puts out a clear-cut stable duplicate of actual radio signals heard on the air, as recommended by all radio code teachers, and the pitch of the signal can be varied to a pleasing tone to suit the student. This feature is an improvement over many previous types of code practice oscillators that quickly tired the student who did not realize that pitch has anything to do with fatigue.

Either a type 37 or a 76 tube may be used, both of which are older varieties that can be salvaged from discarded sets, and are commonly found in radio experimenters' junk boxes. The audio transformer and 20-ohm rheostat are of the same noncritical order. If a 20-ohm rheostat is not at hand a 15-ohm, 1-watt, wire-wound fixed resistor can be used but, of course, this will eliminate the adjustable-pitch feature. A schematic circuit diagram showing a bottom view of the tube socket connections appears in Fig. 1. The simplified wiring diagram, Fig. 4, and photos B and D are top views of the completed unit. Any insulated scrap copper wire, even ordinary bell wire, may be used for the connections to the various parts which are mounted on a thin piece of board so that the key will not be raised any higher than absolutely necessary above the top of the operating table.

Designed as a compact portable assembly to work on any 6-volt battery, the unit is independent of power lines and can be used with a car storage bat-

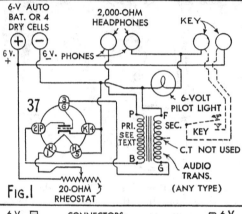

Fig. 1

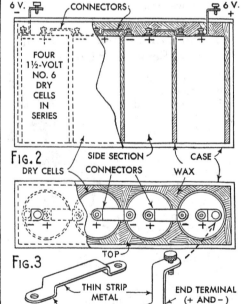

Fig. 2 DRY CELLS

Fig. 3

OSCILLATOR for STUDENTS

tery, a 6-volt "hot shot" battery or four No. 6 dry cells in series. A handy and compact portable dry-cell assembly, well protected from dampness, is detailed in Figs. 2 and 3. This 6-volt unit, suggested by L. B. Robbins W1AFQ, consists of four dry cells connected in series in a suitable container which is then sealed with a black wax compound obtained by breaking up an old B-battery and melting the wax. If a metal case is used, it should be lined with cardboard and cardboard separators placed between the cells. Solder the connecting strips to the battery terminals before pouring in the sealing compound. Positive and negative battery connections are then made with short leads to the clips.

To operate the oscillator only, as shown in photo C, unscrew the pilot light bulb ¼ turn in the hooded dash-light socket. The headphones can be any 2,000 to 4,000-ohm magnetic type; do not use phones of the crystal variety as the tube plate supply continuity is through the earphone circuit. Depress the key and set the rheostat to the desired pitch; it will be noted that the unit can be made to stop oscillating by setting the rheostat at maximum or minimum, however an in-between setting will be found to give a pleasing pitch. It may be necessary to reverse the leads to the primary of the audio transformer to make the tube oscillate. For blinker-light code signals the key can be extended across the table, as indicated in sketch A; tighten the light bulb, and remove the oscillator tube.

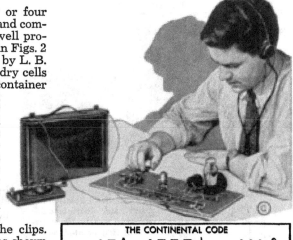

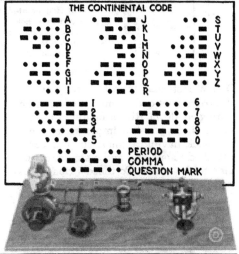

THE CONTINENTAL CODE

A ·—	J ·———
B —···	K —·—
C —·—·	L ·—··
D —··	M ——
E ·	N —·
F ··—·	O ———
G ——·	P ·——·
H ····	Q ——·—
I ··	R ·—·

S ···
T —
U ··—
V ···—
W ·——
X —··—
Y —·——
Z ——··

1 ·————	6 —····
2 ··———	7 ——···
3 ···——	8 ———··
4 ····—	9 ————·
5 ·····	0 —————

·· ·· ·· PERIOD
—·—·— COMMA
··——·· QUESTION MARK

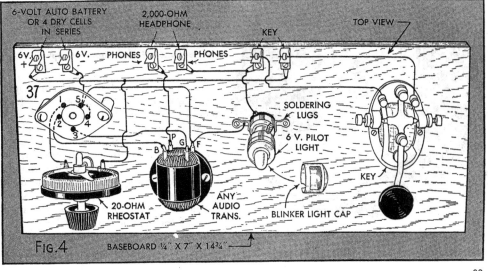

6-VOLT AUTO BATTERY OR 4 DRY CELLS IN SERIES

2,000-OHM HEADPHONE

KEY

TOP VIEW

6V. + — 6V. — PHONES — PHONES — KEY

37

SOLDERING LUGS

6 V. PILOT LIGHT

KEY

20-OHM RHEOSTAT

ANY AUDIO TRANS.

BLINKER LIGHT CAP

FIG. 4   BASEBOARD ¼" X 7" X 14¾"

SIMPLE MODELS PROVE

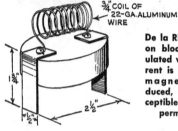
De la Rive's floater: Coil on block floats in acidulated water. Slight current is generated and a magnetic field is produced, making coil susceptible to influence of a permanent magnet

acidulated, say with sulphuric acid, ½ oz. to water, 1 qt. As acid burns, handle it with great care. If you should happen to get some on the skin, wash off immediately under running water and if you get some on clothes apply a strong solution of ordinary baking soda in water at once. Put the float in the acid solution, which should be in a glass jar, and a slight generation of electric current will result, the current flowing through the coil and producing a magnetic field. When you hold a strong permanent magnet near the float, the two magnetic fields will interact and one pole of the permanent magnet will repel one end of the coil and thus the movements of the float can be controlled.

FEW instruments in the study of electromagnetic dynamics are as fascinating as de la Rive's floater, Fig. 1. It consists of a paraffin-impregnated wooden block having a small strip of copper attached to one end and a similar strip of zinc to the other. To these strips a small coil of light wire is connected. The float is placed in water that has been slightly

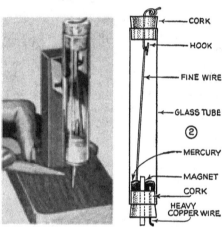
From Faraday: Wire in tube moves around magnet at bottom if direct current is applied

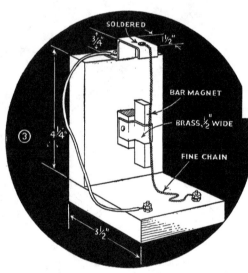
Hanging chain that conducts current is repelled or attracted to magnet in this demonstration

The principles of the electric motor were investigated by Faraday with a model like that shown in Fig. 2. To make it, get a glass tube. A short piece of ⅛-in. drill rod is hardened by heating until red and quickly immersing in oil. Then it is magnetized by bringing one end in contact with one pole of a strong permanent magnet. A wire suspended from a hook is free to move around the magnet and the lower end of the wire should just barely contact the mercury. When direct current is

BASIC ELECTRICAL LAWS

passed through this instrument the wire will rotate continuously.

Another demonstration can be made with the device shown in Fig. 3. Hang or suspend a fine chain near a bar magnet. When a heavy current passes through the chain, one end of it will be attracted to the magnet and the other end will be repelled. Reversing the current reverses the effect. This proves that wires carrying current act like magnets.

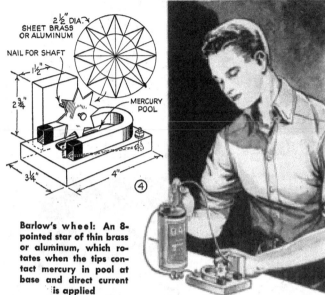

Barlow's wheel: An 8-pointed star of thin brass or aluminum, which rotates when the tips contact mercury in pool at base and direct current is applied

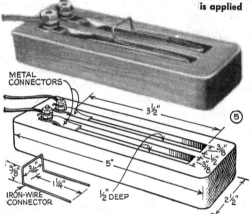

Used by Ampere: Current passing through device makes wire bridge float away from binding posts

Barlow's wheel, Fig. 4, creates much interest. An eight-pointed star of thin sheet aluminum or brass, is mounted on a nail so that it turns easily. As it turns, the points of the star must barely touch the surface of a small pool of mercury. A large permanent magnet is placed as shown. The star will rotate when current from a dry cell is applied. Reversing the current will reverse the rotation.

Fig. 5 shows an interesting instrument once employed by Ampere. Two rectangular troughs to contain mercury are

cut in a piece of wood. Two small pieces of sheet brass or copper wire connect the mercury to binding posts to which a dry cell is connected. Connection between the troughs is made by a piece of No. 22 iron or copper wire bent as shown, which will float on the surface of the mercury. When current is sent

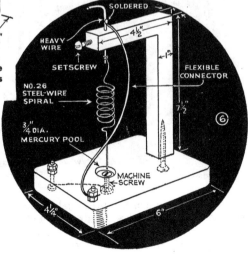

Vibrating coil shortens and lengthens when its lower tip makes and breaks contact with mercury

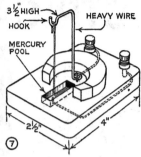

Somewhat similar to the device in Fig. 6. Instead of a coil, a piece of wire vibrates upon making and breaking contact with mercury when connected to direct current

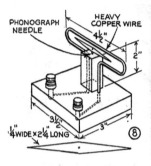

Perfectly balanced on a phonograph needle, a magnetized needle of sheet iron will respond, the extent of movement varying with current applied through coil surrounding it

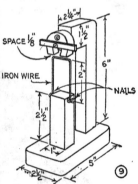

Pivoted iron-wire yoke vibrates like a spring when snapped but stops when another magnet is held close

vibrating spiral, Fig. 6. Make the coil of No. 26-ga. wire, experimenting a bit to get the proper distance between the turns. The top end of the coil is connected to the iron adjusting wire and the bottom just touches the surface of the small pool of mercury. When direct current passes through the coil, the attraction between the turns contracts it and breaks the connection to the mercury. The coil then again relaxes and the effect is repeated at high speed.

In Fig. 7 a length of light wire is suspended between the poles of a permanent magnet so that its tip contacts a small pool of mercury. When a direct current passes through the wire, it will vibrate, making and breaking the contact at the surface of the mercury. The direction of the motion taken by the wire may be reversed by reversing the direction of the electric current. In Fig. 8 a magnetized needle made of sheet iron moves in a loop formed of No. 8 or 10-ga. copper wire. The needle must be perfectly balanced on the point of a phonograph needle. When even a weak current passes through the loop, the needle will respond, the extent of its movement varying with the strength of the current passing through the loop. The simple instrument shown in Fig. 9 has a small yoke of iron wire arranged so that it is free to rotate on two nails that serve as bearings. Normally, the magnet will hold the yoke in the position shown. If the yoke is pulled away from the magnet and released, it will snap back and vibrate violently for a moment much like a spring. Bring the right pole of another magnet near it while it is acting in this way and it will stop.

through this device, a mutual self-repulsion takes place in the circuit, and, being free to move, the wire bridge responds by moving away from the binding posts.

Magnetic forces are actually set up between the turns of any coil carrying an electric current, which is proved by Roget's

❡ Old tooth-brush handles can be shaped to form letter openers, fingernail cleaners, cuticle sticks and many other articles.

Make a Leather Case to Carry Your Camera

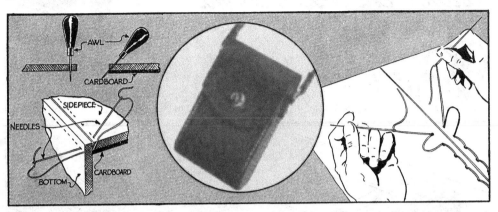

It's no trick to make an attractive carrying case for your camera that will last indefinitely. Tan cowhide ⁹⁄₃₂ in. thick is the best material. To make a case, first measure the camera and cut out the pieces. As the front, back and ends are all in one piece, you can get the measurement by wrapping a tape measure around the camera lengthwise, allowing 2½ in. additional for a flap. Allow ⅜ in. additional in width. Also allow ⅛ in. additional length on the two side pieces. Next cut two pieces of cardboard to the shape of the side pieces and glue them to the flesh side of the leather. The cardboard reinforces the sides. Next, with a bluntly-pointed hardwood stick, impress a line around the leather pieces ⁹⁄₃₂ in. from the edges to serve as guide lines in laying out the holes for stitching. A few additional lines can be made for decoration if desired. Lay out the holes, spacing them ³⁄₁₆ in. apart and punch them with an awl. Note how this is done in the left-hand details. The holes are made vertically in the main part of the case and at a slant in the side pieces. To begin sewing, cut 1¼ yards of thread and use a needle at each end. First sew the left side piece to the main part, starting at hole No. 1 and pass both needles through each successive hole. When you finish, one needle will have to pass through the last hole twice so that the thread can be tied inside the case.

Donkey Guards Your Door

Here's a novel door stop that you can make in an hour or so. It is sawed out of ¼-in. plywood and is painted black with the exception of the feet, nose and eyes, which are white. A couple of rubber-head tacks form the pupils for the eyes. A wedge-shaped piece to slip under the door to hold it is screwed to the rear side near the bottom as indicated in the detail. A piece of small wire coiled and inserted into a small hole drilled in the animal serves as a tail.

—Harold Boquist, Chicago.

A wedge-shaped piece screwed to the rear side of the donkey slips under the door to hold it

MECHANICAL ARTIST
draws endless designs

(1)

(2)

By Walter E. Burton

BY MAKING simple adjustments on the position of the writing arm of this drawing device, you can produce circular designs without limit, some examples of which are shown in Fig. 1. The parts you need to build this gadget, and their arrangement, are shown in Figs. 2 and 6. Four wooden pulleys are mounted on a large baseboard, which may be a drawing board or a piece of plywood. These should be grooved to take a V-belt, leather belting or any kind of homemade belt about 72 in. long. The largest pulley, which is 10 in. in diameter, provides the writing surface, paper being fastened to it with thumbtacks. The smallest pulley, 5 in. in diameter, is provided with a knob so that it can be used as a crank. The other two pulleys, A and B, Fig. 6, are used to guide the writing arm and for this purpose a number of holes are drilled in one side of each as indicated, to take a small pin on the end of the writing arm.

Although the drawings indicate a length of ⅜-in. steel rod for use as a writing arm, you can substitute a piece of maple dowel of larger diameter, which will be fully as serviceable and just as rigid. One end has a pin, as already mentioned, to engage

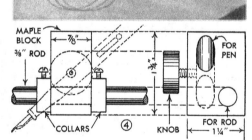

guide wheels A and B, and the other end is fitted to a pivot block which is carried on a rocker arm mounted on a strip of wood that slides back and forth between two guides, and can be locked in any position. A fountain-pen holder, detailed in Figs. 3 and 4, is mounted on the arm and is held in place, after being adjusted to position, by means of two collars of maple. Drilling a hole to take the fountain pen

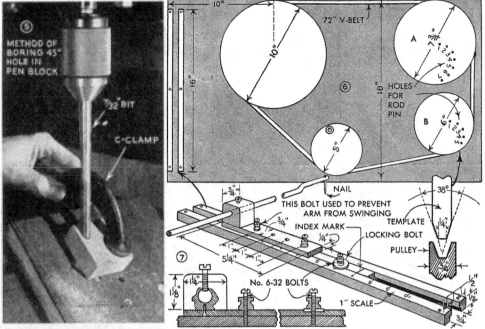

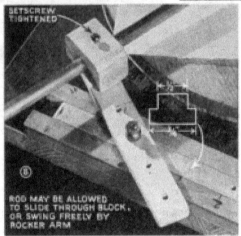

can be done by hand with a wood auger, or on a drillpress as shown in Fig. 5, the size hole being determined by the size of the fountain pen to be used. A thumb-screw can be provided to hold the pen tightly in place.

Details of the writing-arm pivot block, rocker arm, slide and guides are contained in Figs. 6, 7 and 8. Notice that the rod should be allowed to slide in the pivot block if the rocker arm is not arranged to swing as in Fig. 7. However, the rod may be held securely in the block if the rocker arm is pivoted as in Fig. 8. Either arrangement will make a difference in the design drawn. The rocker arm is attached to a guide that moves between two strips to which it can be clamped by means of a locking screw. There is practically no limit to the number of adjustments that can be made at this end of the writing arm, which in conjunction with the holes in the guide wheels, provide still further possibilities.

Holder for Jar of Salmon Eggs Slips Over Trouser Belt

The problem of carrying a jar of salmon-egg fish bait so that it is easy to get at is solved with this simple holder, which slips over your trouser belt. Take an ordinary clothespin and 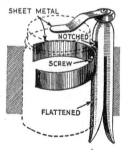 screw a couple of strips of heavy sheet metal or spring steel to it as indicated, making the top one so that it pivots easily. Then cut a notch in the pin just above the circular metal strip to take the edge of the jar lid. When you want to remove some of the eggs, just swing the pivoted metal piece to one side and remove the jar lid.—Lamar Ferguson, Camas, Wash.

By LESTER LEHNHERR

ANY neighborhood group of lively boys and girls can build this outdoor theater and originate among themselves a cast of characters and suitable props for spectacular productions of stage "dramas" and hair-raising mysteries. The simplicity of materials and their availability dispose of the money problem right at the start.

Almost any sort of lumber or materials can be utilized for the stage, Figs. 1 and 2. The frame which forms the arch, or proscenium opening as it is called, Fig. 3, should be of pine 2 by 4-in. stock. Two pieces 7 ft. long and two 8 ft. long are required. Once you have decided on the location, you can set up the frame, anchoring it with either of the two methods shown in Fig. 3.

The frames for the screens are of lighter wood so that they can be moved easily. Four screen panels form the front of the theater; two 3 ft. wide and 7 ft. high, and two 2½ ft. wide and 6 ft. high. See the lower detail in the plan view, Fig. 2. For the stage scenery, two pairs of screens 5 ft. high and one pair 6 ft. high are sufficient to start. They can be either hinged or hooked together as shown in the details in Fig. 1.

After the frames are made, they can be covered with unbleached muslin tacked on and then shrunk and stiffened by painting it with thin glue sizing. Lacking funds for the muslin, corrugated mattress cartons can be used. These make splendid scene panels when merely tacked to the wood frames and painted. Regular wallpaper may be applied to the panels instead of painting them. One of the group is sure to find several rolls of leftover wallpaper in an attic.

If no cartons of any kind are available, newspapers can be used. Heavy sheets of the right size are made by laying several thicknesses of overlapped newspapers together with flour paste or clothes starch as a binder, Fig. 7. The process is continued, layer upon layer, until the whole built-up sheet is ⅛ in. thick or more. In a day or two the starch or paste will have dried and you have a stiff, strong sheet to cover the frame. When painted and decorated it is not possible to tell that these sheets are

THEATER for Young Actors

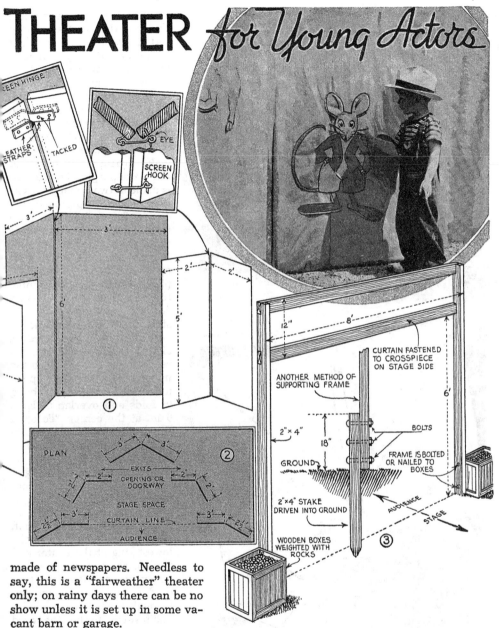

SCREEN HINGE

LEATHER STRAPS — TACKED

EYE

SCREEN HOOK

3'

3'

6'

5'

2'

2'

PLAN

①

②

EXITS

2'

3'

2'

2'

OPENING OR DOORWAY

3'

2'

STAGE SPACE

2½

CURTAIN LINE

3'

2½

AUDIENCE

12"

8'

CURTAIN FASTENED TO CROSSPIECE ON STAGE SIDE

ANOTHER METHOD OF SUPPORTING FRAME

6'

2"×4"

18"

BOLTS

GROUND

FRAME IS BOLTED OR NAILED TO BOXES

2"×4" STAKE DRIVEN INTO GROUND

AUDIENCE

STAGE

③

WOODEN BOXES WEIGHTED WITH ROCKS

made of newspapers. Needless to say, this is a "fairweather" theater only; on rainy days there can be no show unless it is set up in some vacant barn or garage.

A front curtain is needed to close the stage opening between acts and, while a pair of white bed sheets or blankets will serve, a much more unusual and really attractive curtain can be made from odd scraps of cloth sewn together in hit-and-miss fashion, that is, without any definite arrangement as to color or pattern, Figs. 4 and 6. If each actor in the company produces a few odd pieces, there will soon be more than enough. Use only materials of about the same relative weight; thin, sheer materials and heavy woolen suitings will not work well in combination. Since most of the materials to be obtained will be very light in color, or small figured with white backgrounds, it's best to dye them. By closely following the directions on the package and with some supervision and assistance by one of the mothers, this can

be done very successfully. The materials first should be sorted into groups according to the color they will take best. Only three packages of dye need be purchased to secure all possible colors; red, yellow, and blue. Green can be obtained by equal amounts of yellow and blue mixed together; red and yellow will make orange, and blue and red make purple. The curtain is made in two equal pieces so that it may be parted in the center. There should be more than enough material to cover the stage opening so the curtain can hang in folds. For an opening 8 ft. wide, two 6-ft. pieces will allow for ample fullness. The tableau-type curtain is, perhaps, the easier style to arrange and looks very effective. The two halves of the curtain are tacked directly to the crosspiece on the upper edge of the stage opening. The halves should hang in folds and overlap at least 6 in. at the center. To open the curtains, wire curtain rings are sewn to the seams on the back-stage side as shown in Fig. 5. A weight, which may be a small cloth bag with a little sand in it, is sewn to the inside of the lower center corner of each half. Heavy cords are tied to the lowest ring at the center and run up through the rings to screw eyes on the frame. One cord is run across the top through screw eyes or staples and fastened to the other cord

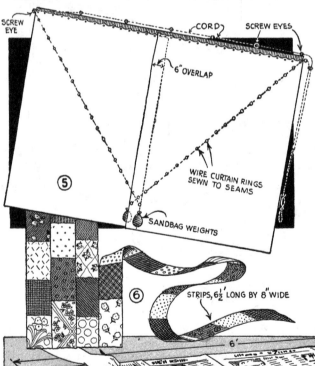

so that both halves will work simultaneously. When the cord is pulled, the two curtains part neatly and draw up to the corners. Upon releasing the cord, the weights cause them to drop back and close the opening.

Now, to make the audience as comfortable as possible is always a good business policy. Therefore, some benches should be provided and a canopy over them will help. See Fig. 9. The canopy is fitted over a frame of wood or pipe and may be altered in size or shape. Benches should vary in height, being higher toward the back, and may be held firmly in place by bolting them to stakes driven into the ground as shown.

For "parent benefit" evening performances when the dads and mothers are invited to the production, a system of lighting is necessary. The arrangement shown in Fig. 8 is easy to install and there are no loose wires or parts to move around. The floodlights are boxes pivoted on angle brackets so they may be turned to direct the beam of light in various directions. They are provided with slides to produce colored lights for special effects; blue for moonlight, green for storm or haunted house, red for fire, amber for sunshine, etc. These slides are formed of two pieces of screen wire taped together with a sheet of colored Cellophane or tissue paper between them. Since large lamps are not necessary on so small a stage, the cur-

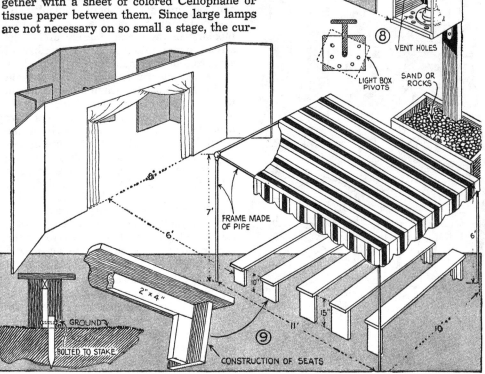

SHELF BRACKET
PIVOTED ON BOLT
⑧
VENT HOLES
LIGHT BOX PIVOTS
SAND OR ROCKS

7'
FRAME MADE OF PIPE
6'
2"x 4"
10"
15"
11'
10'
6'
GROUND
BOLTED TO STAKE
⑨
CONSTRUCTION OF SEATS

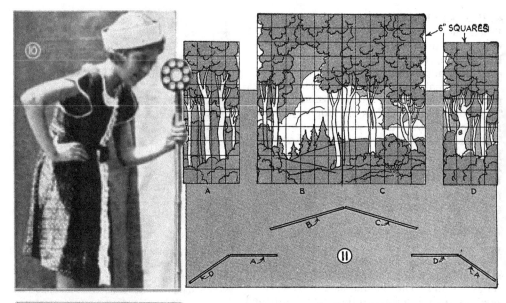

6" SQUARES

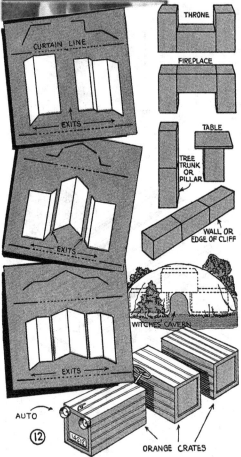

THRONE

FIREPLACE

TABLE

TREE TRUNK OR PILLAR

WALL OR EDGE OF CLIFF

WITCHES CAVERN

CURTAIN LINE

EXITS

EXITS

EXITS

AUTO

ORANGE CRATES

rent can be brought from a near source with rubber-covered extension cord.

A suggested design is given in Fig. 11 for the exterior or scenery which can be painted on one side of the scene panels used for the interior setting, that is, the screens shown back in Fig. 1. The drawing can be enlarged without difficulty by sketching squares on the panels before blocking-in the scene. Merely divide the screen panel into the same number of squares that the small drawing has. Then, starting in one corner of the panel, draw in all the lines that the small drawing has in the corresponding square. This is quite easy to do and when all the squares have been copied, an enlarged sketch of the small drawing results. Paint in bright colors, using simple broad strokes to create the proper atmosphere. Don't attempt to make the scene realistic and detailed. Dry colors can be mixed with whiting or cold-water paint, to make a very clean and economical paint. Figs. 10 and 12 suggest a number of props and ways to arrange the screens to utilize them. Young actors with a lively imagination will be able to build up others to suit special requirements of the play or dialogue. For example in Fig. 10, a few disks of cardboard, a curtain pole and a block of wood make a realistic microphone. Three orange crates, an old steering wheel and two headlights form an automobile and so on.

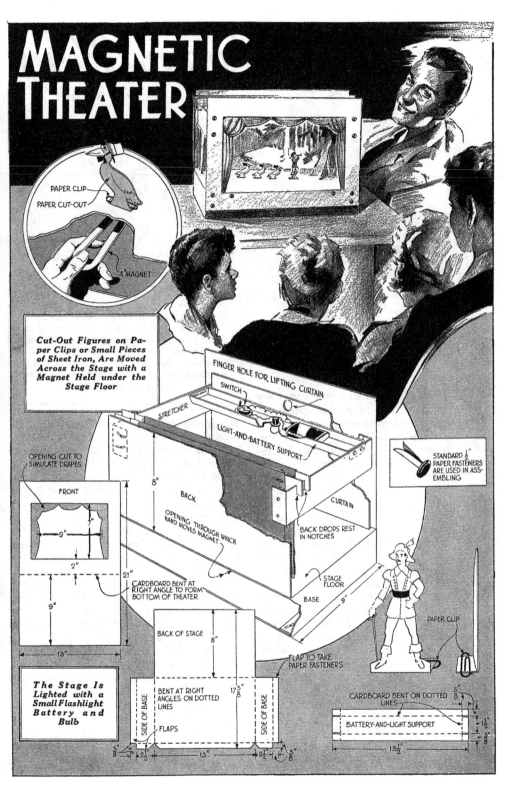

MAGNETIC THEATER

PAPER CLIP

PAPER CUT-OUT

4" MAGNET

Cut-Out Figures on Paper Clips or Small Pieces of Sheet Iron, Are Moved Across the Stage with a Magnet Held under the Stage Floor

FINGER HOLE FOR LIFTING CURTAIN

SWITCH

STRETCHER

LIGHT-AND-BATTERY SUPPORT

STANDARD ½" PAPER FASTENERS ARE USED IN ASSEMBLING

OPENING CUT TO SIMULATE DRAPES

8"

FRONT

BACK

CURTAIN

OPENING THROUGH WHICH HAND MOVES MAGNET

BACK DROPS REST IN NOTCHES

9"

4"

2"

21"

CARDBOARD BENT AT RIGHT ANGLE TO FORM BOTTOM OF THEATER

STAGE FLOOR

9"

BASE

PAPER CLIP

BACK OF STAGE

8"

FLAP TO TAKE PAPER FASTENERS

13"

9"

The Stage Is Lighted with a Small Flashlight Battery and Bulb

SIDE OF BASE

BENT AT RIGHT ANGLES ON DOTTED LINES

17 5/8"

SIDE OF BASE

CARDBOARD BENT ON DOTTED LINES

FLAPS

BATTERY-AND-LIGHT SUPPORT

5/8"

2½"

13"

2½"

5/8"

13½"

95

Small Gas Engine Runs

By FLOYD M. MIX

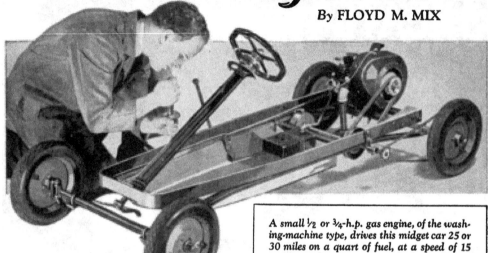

A small ½ or ¾-h.p. gas engine, of the washing-machine type, drives this midget car 25 or 30 miles on a quart of fuel, at a speed of 15 to 20 m.p.h. Operation of both clutch and brake by one lever makes control easy, while pneumatic tires and long, soft springs assure a smooth ride. Construction is simplified by using old auto parts

WITH this midget car you can have plenty of fun at a safe speed. Its simplified control mechanism makes starting and stopping both easy and positive, while its size—58-in. wheelbase and 28½-in. tread—will allow sufficient room for you to be seated comfortably.

The car can be built with ordinary hand tools, and there is no machine work. Only a few parts call for brazing, which can be done at your local machine shop. The frame is the logical place to start. By referring to Fig. 1, you will find that two 61-in. lengths of ⅛ by 2-in. angle iron are needed. The lower right-hand detail shows how one half of the angle iron is cut away, bent and brazed to form the front cross member of the frame. Another piece of angle iron is bolted or brazed on to form the rear cross member. The sides, which are parallel at the rear, have a slight bend as indicated so that they taper toward the front. In drilling holes in the framework, take care to get the dimensions accurate. The frame cross members come next. Note that a ⅝-in. bushing is brazed to the center member. This is used to hold the brake mechanism. Next, a ¾-in. shaft and the cams for tilting the motor are installed,

which should be done before the frame crosspieces are bolted in place; otherwise you will have trouble in getting these parts assembled. Spring steel 1½ in. wide and ¼ in. thick is used for the spring leaves. In the detail drawings, Figs. 1 and 2, you will note there are two bends in each leaf. The springs are not curved uniformly throughout the length. One simple method of making the bends is to heat the metal with a blowtorch just at the point of the bend. After the metal is brought to a dull red, lock it in a vise and quickly bend it to the required radius. Use the same procedure in making all the bends. It is also necessary to draw the temper at the points where the holes are to be drilled. To harden, re-heat at all points and quench in cold water. This method is not orthodox but will serve the purpose. You can save time and insure a true temper by having the job done at a shop equipped for handling work of this kind.

For the front axle and steering gear, Fig. 4, you will need a model-T Ford steering column, brake rods to be used for drag and tie rods, and a couple of brake clevises

this MIDGET CAR

from a four-cylinder Dodge. These parts are usually available at auto-wrecking yards. Steering knuckles are bent from ⅜-in. malleable iron, to dimensions given. Wheel spindles, cut from ⅝-in. cold-rolled steel shafting, are brazed to the knuckles and the axle yokes are brazed into ¾-in. iron-pipe housing. The steering-wheel housing is shortened to 22¾ in. and the steering rod is sawed off accordingly. In making the installation, the column is inverted and the flange is bent to a right angle. Wheels which are recommended for this car are equipped with ball bearings and 2.50 x 12.75-in. pneumatic tires. Two and four-ply tires are available.

Next comes the rear-wheel assembly. Only one wheel serves as a driver as indicated in Fig. 5. This method eliminates a complicated differential, and numerous tests have proved it to be entirely satisfactory. Great care must be taken in drilling holes in the hardwood disk so that the bicycle sprocket will be concentric with the disk. Both rear wheels run loosely on a ⅝-in. axle, cut from cold-rolled steel shafting. They are held by the axle housing on the inside, and castellated nuts, which have been properly keyed, on the outside. Details of the control lever and braking mechanism are given in Figs. 2 and 3. When the lever is pushed forward the motor is tilted upward to tighten the drive belt and the car moves ahead. When the lever is pulled back the belt is slackened and the brake applied. To hold the drive shaft in place, you will need two brackets, as dimensioned in the upper left detail of Fig. 2. These can be cast from small patterns, or something suitable may be picked up at an auto junk yard. The idea is to provide good bearings for the ⅝-in. shaft. While you are at the junk yard, get a 4⅝-in. Dodge fan pulley and a model-T Ford brake band. Fig. 3 shows clearly how these parts should be assembled on the drive shaft.

For the floor pan, you will need a piece

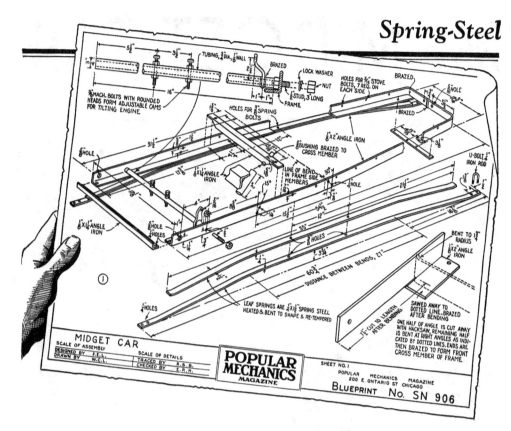

of No. 22-ga. sheet iron 24 in. wide and about 44 in. long. Bend it to shape as indicated in one of the details, Fig. 2. Place the metal in position on the inside of the frame and drill holes to take 3/16-in. stove bolts. Before going further, it is a good idea to braze the corner seams, as this tends to strengthen the floor. Now put in the stove bolts, using a small lock washer on each to prevent loosening. When the chassis has been completed, the engine is installed so you can take it around the block a few times before going ahead with the body. The base to which the engine is bolted may be made of 1½-in. hardwood. Drill the piece edgewise at one end to take the 5/8-in. shaft on which the engine is pivoted, as in Fig. 2. This arrangement permits the engine to tilt easily, yet is sufficiently rigid to prevent vibration. Another method of making such a base is to cut a suitable piece of fairly heavy sheet metal wide enough to permit two opposite edges to be bent over at right angles and drilled to fit the shaft. Slide the engine on the

shaft until the pulley alines with the drive-shaft pulley, mark on each side and drill for cotter keys, which hold the engine in place. A small rectangular-shaped gas tank is installed just ahead of the second frame cross member, as indicated in Fig. 2. It is important that this be slung low enough to fit under the seat, dimensioned in Fig. 5. Start up the engine and do the necessary experimenting and adjusting to get the various parts lined up. A gas-control lever is not required as the speed of the engine is automatically taken care of by an adjustable governor.

When tests prove that everything works satisfactorily, you can start on the body. This is built in two parts, and, as there are alternate designs, you can use either a metal or cloth covering. The cloth-covered body is perhaps the easiest to build, although it is not as desirable as a sheet-metal body, which can be finished up to make the car look like a real racer. On the metal body, Figs. 7 to 9, it is advisable to build up the rear section first. Before

Leaves Fitted to a Sturdy Angle-Iron Chassis

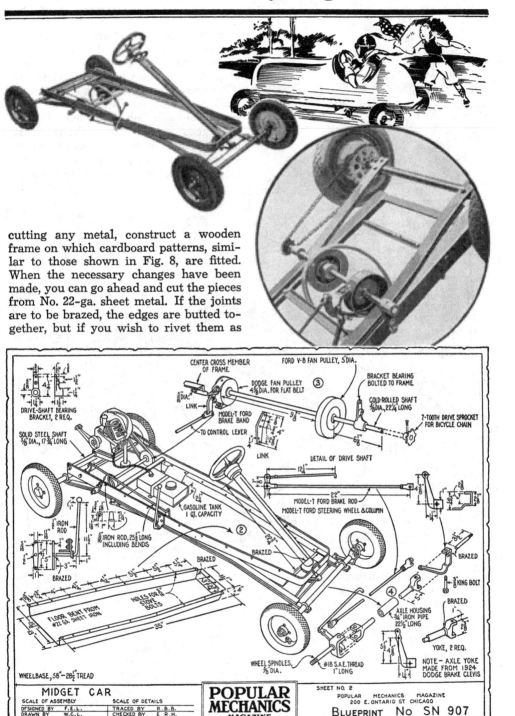

cutting any metal, construct a wooden frame on which cardboard patterns, similar to those shown in Fig. 8, are fitted. When the necessary changes have been made, you can go ahead and cut the pieces from No. 22-ga. sheet metal. If the joints are to be brazed, the edges are butted together, but if you wish to rivet them as

DRIVE-SHAFT BEARING BRACKET, 2 REQ.

SOLID STEEL SHAFT ⅝ DIA., 17¾ LONG

CENTER CROSS MEMBER OF FRAME

FORD V-8 FAN PULLEY, 5"DIA.

DODGE FAN PULLEY 4⅝DIA. FOR FLAT BELT

BRACKET BEARING BOLTED TO FRAME

COLD-ROLLED SHAFT ⅝DIA., 22¼ LONG

7-TOOTH DRIVE SPROCKET FOR BICYCLE CHAIN

LINK

MODEL-T FORD BRAKE BAND

TO CONTROL LEVER

LINK

DETAIL OF DRIVE SHAFT

⅝ IRON ROD

GASOLINE TANK 1 QT. CAPACITY

⅝ IRON ROD, 25½ LONG INCLUDING BENDS

22"
MODEL-T FORD BRAKE ROD
MODEL-T FORD STEERING WHEEL & COLUMN

BRAZED

BRAZED

BRAZED

BRAZED

KING BOLT

BRAZED

BRAZED

FLOOR BELT FROM #22 GA. SHEET IRON

HOLES FOR STOVE BOLTS

35"

AXLE HOUSING ¾ IRON PIPE 22½ LONG

YOKE, 2 REQ.

NOTE — AXLE YOKE MADE FROM 1924 DODGE BRAKE CLEVIS

WHEEL SPINDLES, ⅞ DIA.

#18 S.A.E. THREAD 1" LONG

WHEELBASE, 58"—28½ TREAD

MIDGET CAR		POPULAR MECHANICS MAGAZINE	SHEET NO. 2
SCALE OF ASSEMBLY	SCALE OF DETAILS		POPULAR MECHANICS MAGAZINE 200 E. ONTARIO ST CHICAGO
DESIGNED BY F.E.L.	TRACED BY R.B.B.		BLUEPRINT No SN 907
DRAWN BY W.C.L.	CHECKED BY E R.H.		

your local garage. During the shaping process, the metal should be annealed at intervals by heating to a dull red with a blowtorch and allowing it to cool slowly. It is a good idea to practice on some rough stock in order to get the experience necessary to do a good job on this part. Use the same general procedure on the front half of the body, Fig. 9. As suggested in the drawing, the lower part should be assembled first, shaping it properly and riveting

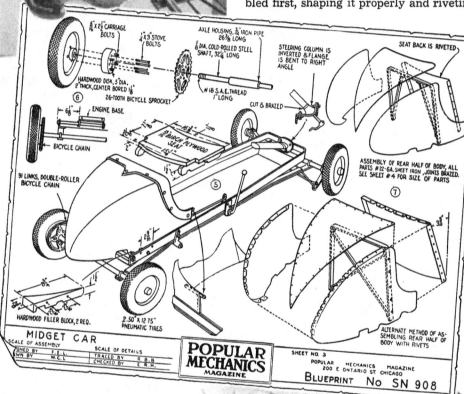

MIDGET CAR

SCALE OF ASSEMBLY

SCALE OF DETAILS

POPULAR MECHANICS MAGAZINE

SHEET NO. 3

POPULAR MECHANICS MAGAZINE
200 E ONTARIO ST. CHICAGO

BLUEPRINT No SN 908

shown in the lower detail, Fig. 7, allow an extra inch of metal on the side pieces to take the rivets. In either case, it is necessary that the three pieces, which comprise the rear half of the body, be shaped as much as possible to the final form before brazing or riveting. A set of fender-straightening irons will help you greatly in doing this work. Perhaps you can borrow a set of these tools from

Alternate Body Designs

it to the frame. Then you can braze the seams and go ahead with the shaping. Hammer out all the dents you can, and even up the bumps with a coarse file. Finish with a fine file and sandpaper.

The chassis is attractive when finished in aluminum, while the body looks best in a bright color, such as red, green or orange. The original car, which was finished in "fire-engine" red, proved to be unusually attractive. For the exact procedure, first

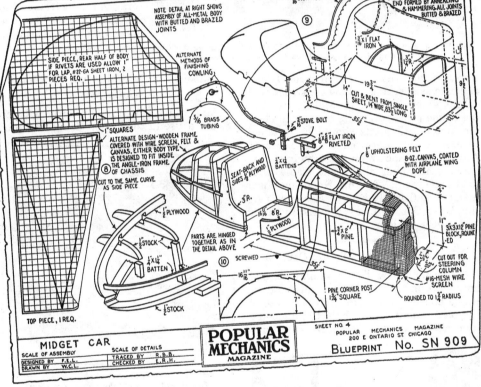

NOTE DETAIL AT RIGHT SHOWS ASSEMBLY OF ALL-METAL BODY WITH BUTTED AND BRAZED JOINTS

TOP IS CUT TO FIT AFTER ASSEMBLY OF LOWER PART, FORWARD END FORMED BY ANNEALING & HAMMERING-ALL JOINTS BUTTED & BRAZED

$\frac{3}{16}$ IRON ROD

SIDE PIECE, REAR HALF OF BODY IF RIVETS ARE USED ALLOW 1" FOR LAP. #22-GA SHEET IRON, 2 PIECES REQ.

ALTERNATE METHODS OF FINISHING COWLING

$\frac{3}{4}$"x1" FLAT $\frac{1}{16}$ IRON

1" SQUARES

$\frac{5}{16}$" BRASS TUBING

ALTERNATE DESIGN-WOODEN FRAME COVERED WITH WIRE SCREEN, FELT & CANVAS, EITHER BODY TYPE, IS DESIGNED TO FIT INSIDE THE ANGLE-IRON FRAME OF CHASSIS

CUT TO THE SAME CURVE AS SIDE PIECE

$\frac{3}{16}$"STOVE BOLT

$\frac{3}{4}$"x$\frac{3}{8}$"FLAT IRON RIVETED

$\frac{1}{8}$" UPHOLSTERING FELT

8-OZ. CANVAS, COATED WITH AIRPLANE WING DOPE

CUT & BENT FROM SINGLE SHEET, 14" WIDE, 83$\frac{1}{2}$" LONG

SEAT-BACK AND SIDES $\frac{1}{2}$" PLYWOOD

$\frac{1}{4}$"x1$\frac{1}{4}$" BATTENS

$\frac{1}{2}$" PLYWOOD

3"R.

PARTS ARE HINGED TOGETHER AS IN THE DETAIL ABOVE

$\frac{1}{2}$"STOCK

$\frac{1}{4}$"x1$\frac{1}{4}$" BATTEN

SCREWED

$\frac{1}{2}$" PLYWOOD

$\frac{1}{4}$"x2" PINE

$\frac{1}{2}$"STOCK

3"x3"x12" PINE BLOCK, ROUNDED

CUT OUT FOR STEERING COLUMN

#16-MESH WIRE SCREEN

PINE CORNER POST 1$\frac{3}{4}$" SQUARE

ROUNDED TO 1$\frac{3}{4}$" RADIUS

TOP PIECE, I REQ.

MIDGET CAR
SCALE OF ASSEMBLY
DESIGNED BY F.E.L.
DRAWN BY W.C.L.
SCALE OF DETAILS
TRACED BY R.B.B.
CHECKED BY E.R.H.

POPULAR MECHANICS MAGAZINE

SHEET NO. 4
POPULAR MECHANICS MAGAZINE
200 E ONTARIO ST CHICAGO

BLUEPRINT No. SN 909

give the body a coat of metal primer. When this is thoroughly dry, sand lightly, then fill all the dents with glazing putty. This material is semi-solid and is worked into the cavities, file marks, etc., with a piece of rubber, such as cut from an old truck tube. Let the putty dry, then even it up with sandpaper. Finish with two or three coats of high-grade enamel, sanding be-

tween coats. Spraying is preferable, but you can do a good job with a brush, if you take plenty of time. Striping will add to the attractiveness of the car. Upholstering on the back of the seat is also suggested. Rubberized cloth, such as used in making auto side curtains is satisfactory for the purpose. A suitable radiator ornament can be purchased from the 5 and 10-cent

Rear Half of Body Is Lifted to Start and Adjust Motor; Strong Air Current from Built-In Flywheel-Type Fan Keeps Motor Cool

small box camera. Thus the view to be included in the picture can be seen through the frame. To make the view finder, cut out a rectangular frame of thin, stiff sheet metal, making the opening about the same size as the picture the camera takes. Then cut out a smaller frame of metal with an opening about ¼ in. square. Mount the frames vertically at the ends of a thin strip of wood of the same length as the camera. Paint the frames dull black and then bind the assembly on the camera with elastic bands.

store. If you wish to use a wood frame and canvas covering, follow constructional details given in Fig. 10. Make sure that the frame pieces are long enough to clear the motor. All joints should be fastened securely with waterproof glue and screws. Although not shown on the drawings, it is possible to cover the wood frame with light sheet metal. For this, No. 26-ga. sheet metal is sufficiently heavy. Because of its simplicity, this method is favored by many midget-car builders.

View Finder for Small Box Camera

A "visual" view finder similar to that now used on many folding hand cameras, which consists of a wire frame the size of the picture and a peep hole to which the user places one eye, is easily made for a

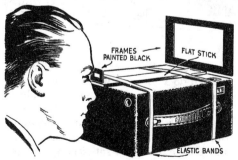

Homemade View Finder for Box Camera Enables You to See Full-Size View of Scene

Shoehorn Is Useful When Handling Insulated Wire

An ordinary metal shoehorn will be found a useful tool when doing odd jobs

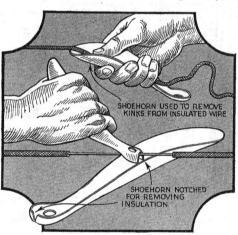

A Metal Shoehorn Will Be Found Handy When Doing Odd Wiring Jobs around the Home

of electrical wiring around your home. Kinked wire can be straightened by pulling it over the rounded trough of the horn as shown in the upper detail, while bared wire can be scraped for soldering if a V-notch is cut in the other end of the horn. If the edges of the notch are sharpened with a file, the notch will be helpful in removing insulation from the wire.

What You Can Do with a COUPLE of WHEELS

With a pair of small balloon wheels, one can build novel vehicles for work and play. The light barrow at the left is less cumbersome than the standard models and is a real convenience for the amateur gardener, while the speedy coaster below will give the children a thrill. Its low center of gravity and powerful brake make it safe

Barrow:
ALL ½" PLYWOOD
FRONT END GALV. LINING
3-CORNERED CLEATS CASEIN GLUED
1½ x 42 OAK HANDLES
45°
50
26
18
30

Coaster:
SEAT
MODEL-T STEERING WHEEL
INNER TUBE STRIPS
STEERING ROD
FOOT REST
FOOT BAR
HARDWOOD BRAKE
HINGES
PIPE BEARING
10" BALLOON WHEEL
5" x ³⁄₃₂" IRON WELDED OR RIVETED
25" 18" 9"
21" 33" 13"

Trailer:
¾" SEAMLESS TUBING 40"
FLAT-IRON HITCH
RUBBER WASHERS
³⁄₈" PLYWOOD BODY
18"
24"
STRAPS
AXLE FASTENING
1½" x 2 x 19 WHITE PINE

A cart to convey food, hot or cold, and beverages from kitchen to garden is illustrated above. The cycling vacationist will get good use from the simple trailer at the right

103

MIDGET TRAILERS

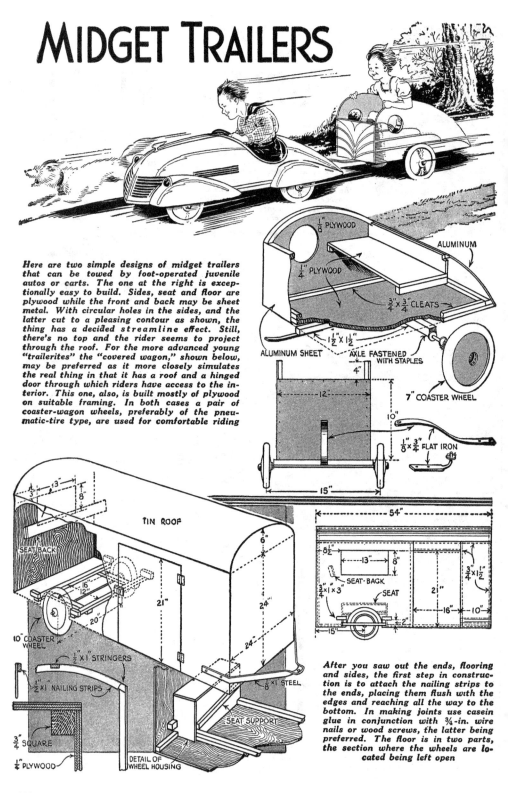

Here are two simple designs of midget trailers that can be towed by foot-operated juvenile autos or carts. The one at the right is exceptionally easy to build. Sides, seat and floor are plywood while the front and back may be sheet metal. With circular holes in the sides, and the latter cut to a pleasing contour as shown, the thing has a decided streamline effect. Still, there's no top and the rider seems to project through the roof. For the more advanced young "trailerites" the "covered wagon," shown below, may be preferred as it more closely simulates the real thing in that it has a roof and a hinged door through which riders have access to the interior. This one, also, is built mostly of plywood on suitable framing. In both cases a pair of coaster-wagon wheels, preferably of the pneumatic-tire type, are used for comfortable riding

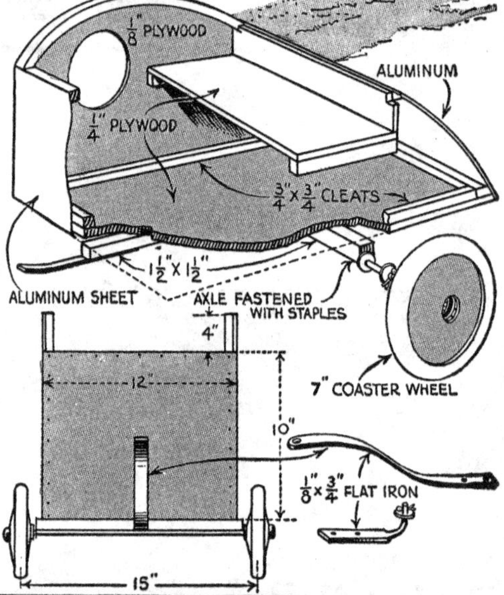

$\frac{1}{8}$" PLYWOOD
ALUMINUM
$\frac{1}{4}$" PLYWOOD
$\frac{3}{4}$"x$\frac{3}{4}$" CLEATS
$1\frac{1}{2}$" X $1\frac{1}{2}$"
ALUMINUM SHEET
AXLE FASTENED WITH STAPLES
4"
12"
10"
7" COASTER WHEEL
$\frac{1}{8}$"x$\frac{3}{4}$" FLAT IRON
15"

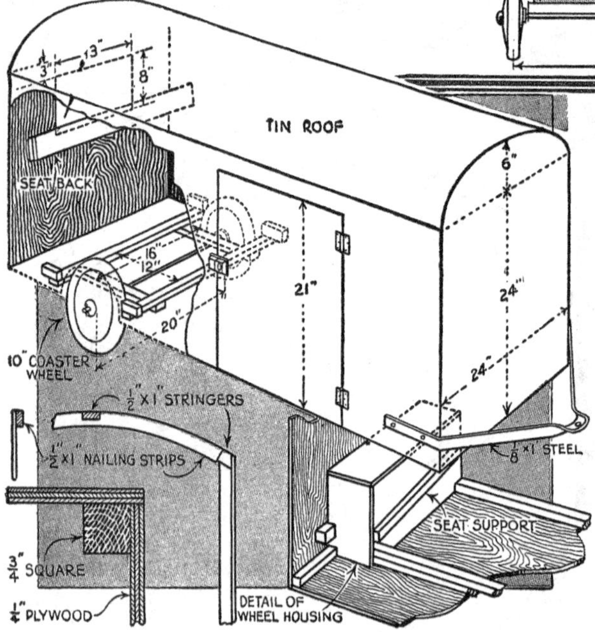

3"
13"
8"
TIN ROOF
SEAT BACK
6"
16"
12"
20"
21"
24"
24"
10" COASTER WHEEL
$\frac{1}{2}$"x1" STRINGERS
$\frac{1}{2}$"x1" NAILING STRIPS
$\frac{1}{8}$"x1" STEEL
SEAT SUPPORT
$\frac{3}{4}$" SQUARE
$\frac{1}{4}$" PLYWOOD
DETAIL OF WHEEL HOUSING

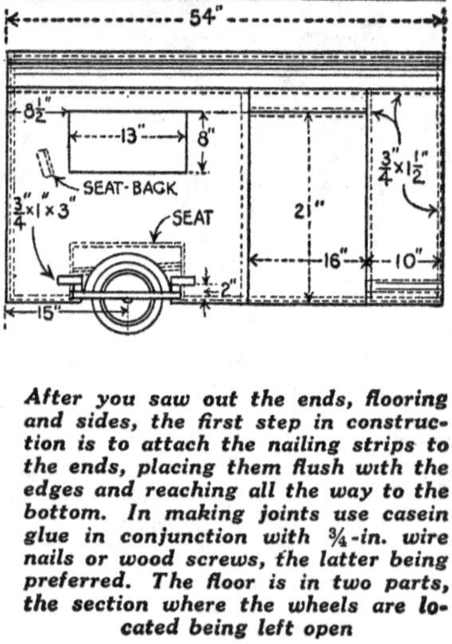

54"
$8\frac{1}{2}$"
13"
8"
$\frac{3}{4}$"x$1\frac{1}{2}$"
SEAT-BACK
$\frac{3}{4}$"x1"x3"
SEAT
21"
16"
10"
2"
15"

After you saw out the ends, flooring and sides, the first step in construction is to attach the nailing strips to the ends, placing them flush with the edges and reaching all the way to the bottom. In making joints use casein glue in conjunction with ¾-in. wire nails or wood screws, the latter being preferred. The floor is in two parts, the section where the wheels are located being left open

Sidewalk Scooters

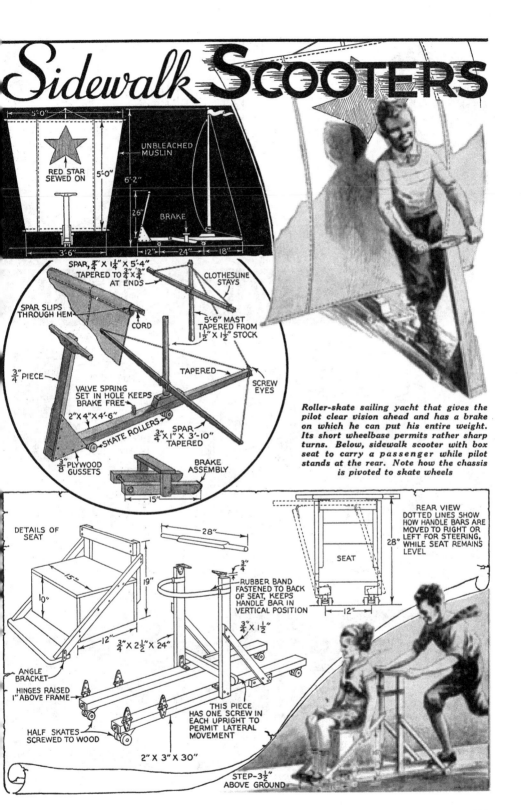

5'-0"

RED STAR SEWED ON

UNBLEACHED MUSLIN

5'-0"

6'-2"

26"

BRAKE

3'-6"

12" — 24" — 18"

SPAR, ¾" X 1¼" X 5'-4" TAPERED TO ¾" X ¾" AT ENDS

CLOTHESLINE STAYS

SPAR SLIPS THROUGH HEM

CORD

5'-6" MAST TAPERED FROM 1½" X 1½" STOCK

¾" PIECE

TAPERED

SCREW EYES

VALVE SPRING SET IN HOLE KEEPS BRAKE FREE

2"X 4"X 4'-6"

SKATE ROLLERS

SPAR ¾" X 1" X 3'-10" TAPERED

⅜" PLYWOOD GUSSETS

BRAKE ASSEMBLY

15"

Roller-skate sailing yacht that gives the pilot clear vision ahead and has a brake on which he can put his entire weight. Its short wheelbase permits rather sharp turns. Below, sidewalk scooter with box seat to carry a passenger while pilot stands at the rear. Note how the chassis is pivoted to skate wheels

DETAILS OF SEAT

28"

REAR VIEW DOTTED LINES SHOW HOW HANDLE BARS ARE MOVED TO RIGHT OR LEFT FOR STEERING, WHILE SEAT REMAINS LEVEL

28"

SEAT

¾"

RUBBER BAND FASTENED TO BACK OF SEAT, KEEPS HANDLE BAR IN VERTICAL POSITION

¾" X 1½"

12"

15"

19"

10"

12"   ¾" X 2½" X 24"

ANGLE BRACKET

HINGES RAISED 1" ABOVE FRAME

THIS PIECE HAS ONE SCREW IN EACH UPRIGHT TO PERMIT LATERAL MOVEMENT

HALF SKATES SCREWED TO WOOD

2" X 3" X 30"

STEP-3½" ABOVE GROUND

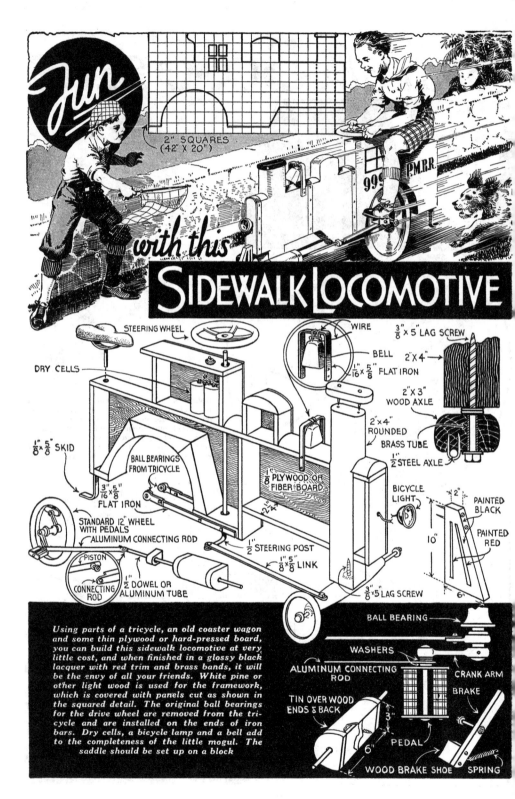

FUN with this SIDEWALK LOCOMOTIVE

2" SQUARES (42" X 20")

STEERING WHEEL

DRY CELLS

WIRE

BELL

$\frac{3}{8}" \times 5"$ LAG SCREW

$\frac{1}{16}" \times \frac{5}{8}"$ FLAT IRON

2" X 4"

2" X 3" WOOD AXLE

2" X 4" ROUNDED

BRASS TUBE

$\frac{1}{2}"$ STEEL AXLE

$\frac{1}{8}" \times \frac{5}{8}"$ SKID

BALL BEARINGS FROM TRICYCLE

$\frac{1}{8}"$ PLYWOOD OR FIBER BOARD

$\frac{3}{16}" \times \frac{5}{8}"$ FLAT IRON

STANDARD 12" WHEEL WITH PEDALS

ALUMINUM CONNECTING ROD

$\frac{1}{2}"$ STEERING POST

$\frac{1}{8}" \times \frac{5}{8}"$ LINK

BICYCLE LIGHT

2"

PAINTED BLACK

10"

PAINTED RED

PISTON

CONNECTING ROD

$\frac{1}{2}"$ DOWEL OR ALUMINUM TUBE

$\frac{3}{8}" \times 5"$ LAG SCREW

6"

BALL BEARING

WASHERS

ALUMINUM CONNECTING ROD

TIN OVER WOOD ENDS & BACK

CRANK ARM

BRAKE

3"

PEDAL

6"

WOOD BRAKE SHOE

SPRING

Using parts of a tricycle, an old coaster wagon and some thin plywood or hard-pressed board, you can build this sidewalk locomotive at very little cost, and when finished in a glossy black lacquer with red trim and brass bands, it will be the envy of all your friends. White pine or other light wood is used for the framework, which is covered with panels cut as shown in the squared detail. The original ball bearings for the drive wheel are removed from the tricycle and are installed on the ends of iron bars. Dry cells, a bicycle lamp and a bell add to the completeness of the little mogul. The saddle should be set up on a block

CARGO STEAMER···
for the junior ship modeler

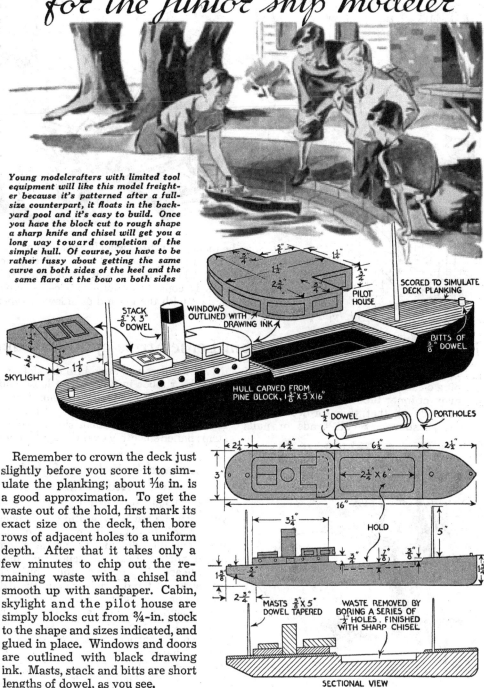

Young modelcrafters with limited tool equipment will like this model freighter because it's patterned after a full-size counterpart, it floats in the backyard pool and it's easy to build. Once you have the block cut to rough shape a sharp knife and chisel will get you a long way toward completion of the simple hull. Of course, you have to be rather fussy about getting the same curve on both sides of the keel and the same flare at the bow on both sides

PILOT HOUSE

SCORED TO SIMULATE DECK PLANKING

STACK $\frac{5}{8}$" X 3" DOWEL

WINDOWS OUTLINED WITH DRAWING INK

BITTS OF $\frac{3}{8}$" DOWEL

SKYLIGHT

HULL CARVED FROM PINE BLOCK, $1\frac{3}{8}$" X 3" X 16"

$\frac{1}{2}$" DOWEL

PORTHOLES

Remember to crown the deck just slightly before you score it to simulate the planking; about $\frac{1}{16}$ in. is a good approximation. To get the waste out of the hold, first mark its exact size on the deck, then bore rows of adjacent holes to a uniform depth. After that it takes only a few minutes to chip out the remaining waste with a chisel and smooth up with sandpaper. Cabin, skylight and the pilot house are simply blocks cut from ¾-in. stock to the shape and sizes indicated, and glued in place. Windows and doors are outlined with black drawing ink. Masts, stack and bitts are short lengths of dowel, as you see.

$2\frac{1}{4}$" · $4\frac{1}{4}$" · $6\frac{1}{4}$" · $2\frac{1}{2}$"

3"

$2\frac{1}{4}$" X 6"

16"

$3\frac{1}{4}$"

HOLD

5"

MASTS $\frac{3}{8}$" X 5" DOWEL TAPERED

WASTE REMOVED BY BORING A SERIES OF $\frac{1}{2}$" HOLES. FINISHED WITH SHARP CHISEL

SECTIONAL VIEW

This Coaster Has Drag Brake for Quick Stops

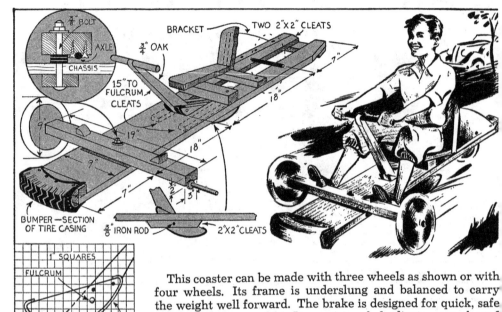

This coaster can be made with three wheels as shown or with four wheels. Its frame is underslung and balanced to carry the weight well forward. The brake is designed for quick, safe stops on steep grades. It consists of duplicate cam-shaped shoes brought into contact with the ground or sidewalk when you pull back on the hand lever.

Non-Slip Feet for Ladder from Loose Strips of Inner Tube

Light ladders can be prevented from slipping on smooth surfaces by fitting folded strips of inner tube into slots cut in the lower ends so that they project a few inches as shown. Small brads or nails driven through the wood into the slots will hold the rubber in place. The loose ends of the strips accommodate themselves to the slope of the surface and will hold the ladder more securely than similar rubber strips nailed smoothly over the ladder ends.

Sun and Rain Proof Labels to Identify Plants

Plant labels that will last for several years can be made by writing with black ink or soft-lead pencil on strips of thin wood and then dipping them in spar varnish or shellac. Less conspicuous and more durable are labels made of zinc. This is cut into strips of the desired size and the data written on them with a mixture of hydrochloric acid, 1 liquid oz., and powdered antimony, 1 oz., the latter being stirred into the acid. A sharp-pointed wood skewer or pointed hardwood twig is used for a pen. The writing will turn black on the zinc and both writing and label will last indefinitely
—John P. Thorn, Elizabeth, N. J.

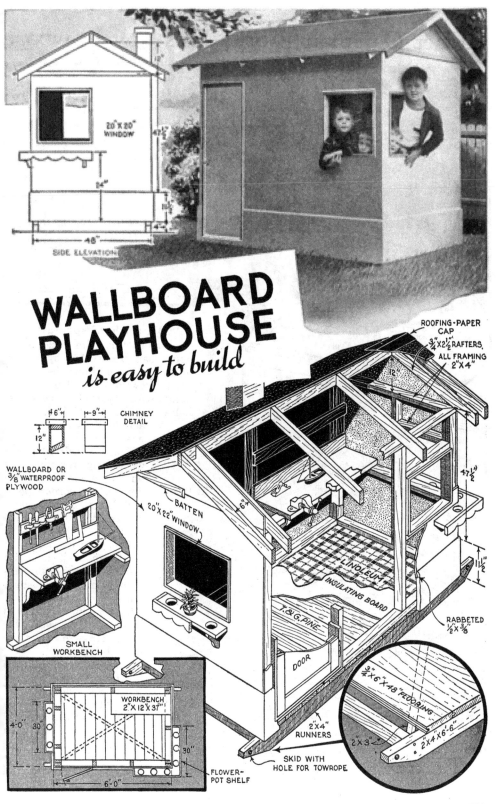

SIDE ELEVATION

20" X 20" WINDOW

47½"

24"

48"

WALLBOARD PLAYHOUSE
is easy to build

CHIMNEY DETAIL

6"

9"

12"

WALLBOARD OR 3/8" WATERPROOF PLYWOOD

BATTEN

20" X 22" WINDOW

6"

ROOFING-PAPER CAP

3/4" X 2½" RAFTERS

ALL FRAMING 2" X 4"

12"

47½"

SMALL WORKBENCH

LINOLEUM

INSULATING BOARD

T. & G. PINE

RABBETED ½" X 3/8"

1½"

WORKBENCH 2" X 12" X 37"

4'-0"

30

30

6'-0"

FLOWER-POT SHELF

DOOR

2" X 4" RUNNERS

SKID WITH HOLE FOR TOWROPE

3/4" X 6" X 48" FLOORING

2" X 4" X 6'-6"

2" X 3"

This PLAYHOUSE

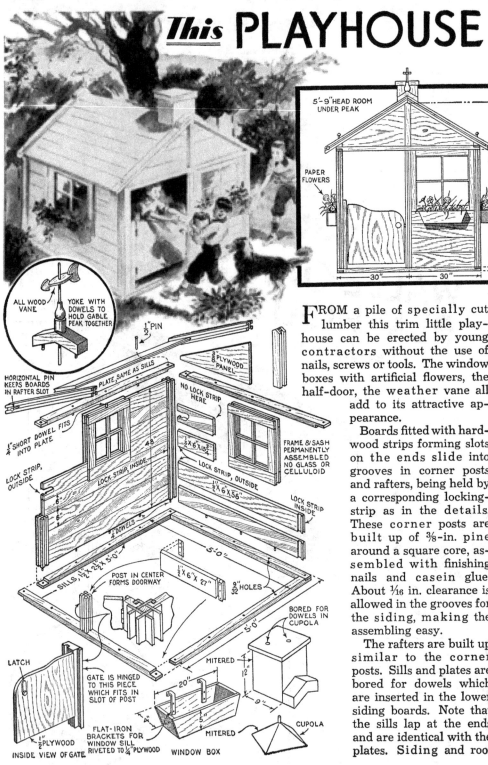

5'-9" HEAD ROOM UNDER PEAK

PAPER FLOWERS

30" | 30"

F ROM a pile of specially cut lumber this trim little playhouse can be erected by young contractors without the use of nails, screws or tools. The window boxes with artificial flowers, the half-door, the weather vane all add to its attractive appearance.

Boards fitted with hardwood strips forming slots on the ends slide into grooves in corner posts and rafters, being held by a corresponding locking-strip as in the details. These corner posts are built up of ⅜-in. pine around a square core, assembled with finishing nails and casein glue. About ¹⁄₁₆ in. clearance is allowed in the grooves for the siding, making the assembling easy.

The rafters are built up similar to the corner posts. Sills and plates are bored for dowels which are inserted in the lower siding boards. Note that the sills lap at the ends and are identical with the plates. Siding and roof

is assembled without nails

boards are ½ by 6-in. pine, with V-bevel and groove as shown. These boards are in three lengths—for the full width of the structure, for half-widths as at the side of the door, and the short ones to go alongside the windows.

The peak of the gable is held together with a wooden yoke, which straddles the ends of the rafters. Two of these yokes are required. Window boxes made of ¼-in. plywood are supported by two flat-iron brackets as shown. The half-door or gate is hinged to a piece which slides down in the slot of the corner post and is hung to swing out. A wooden latch, as shown, fits into the slot of the other door post.

Window frames are grooved at the sides and across the bottom to fit over the siding, and at the top a short dowel is set into a hole bored in the plate. The central framework with the mullions is of $9/16$-in. material while the outside framing is of ⅜-in. stock. No glass or celluloid panes are used. Study of the details will show that the design can be changed easily. For example, you can make duplicate parts for two structures, join these end to end with a special beam under the central rafters and you have a schoolhouse. In the original design the parts were left unpainted, as the young builder usually likes to work with new boards. Of course, if the house is to be erected outdoors and exposed to wet weather, it should be varnished or painted.

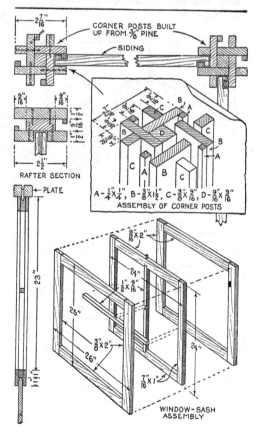

111

Wheeled "SNACK SHACK"
rolls to profit spots

STATIONED at any spot where refreshments can be sold, this gay-colored booth will pay you dividends. Balloon-type pneumatic wheels equipped with roller bearings and sturdy axles are used. Framing is covered at the bottom and roof with hard-pressed board. From the counter to the roof the covering is wire-glass to offer weather protection without shutting off the light. There is a door at the rear and two of the front frames are fitted with removable or hinged sash through which customers are served.

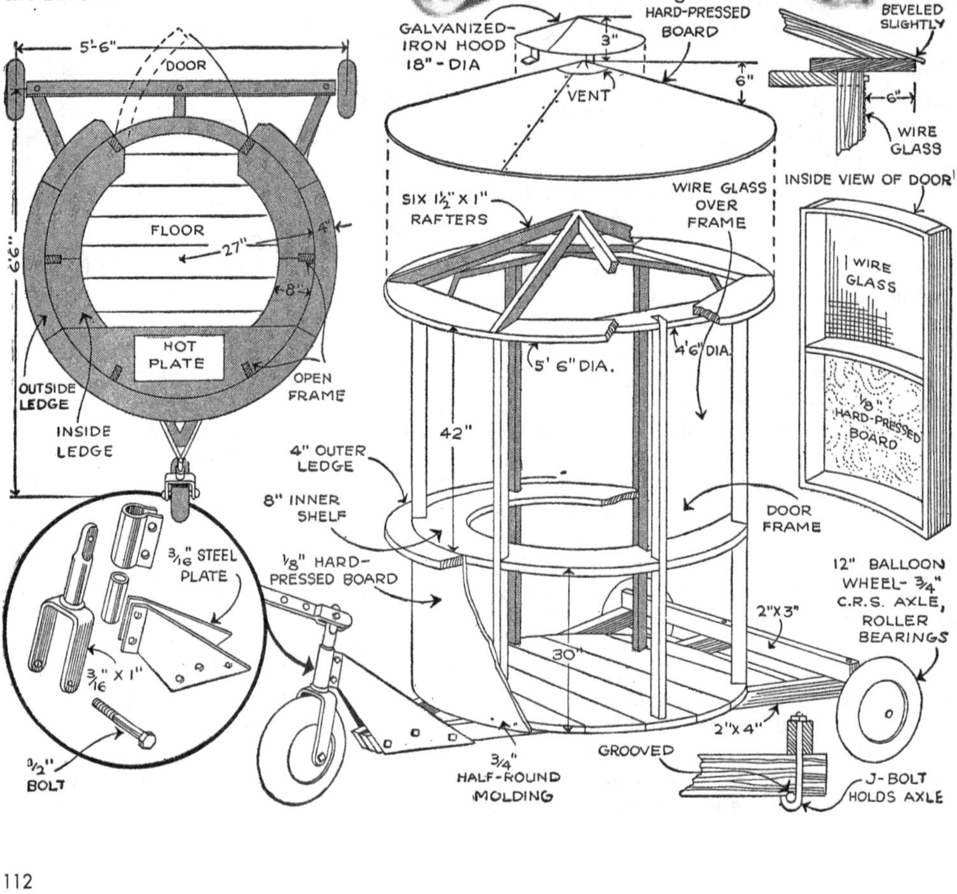

GALVANIZED-IRON HOOD 18"-DIA

1/8" HARD-PRESSED BOARD

3"

VENT

6"

BEVELED SLIGHTLY

6"

WIRE GLASS

5'-6"

DOOR

6'-6"

FLOOR

27"

4"

8"

HOT PLATE

OUTSIDE LEDGE

OPEN FRAME

INSIDE LEDGE

SIX 1/2" X 1" RAFTERS

WIRE GLASS OVER FRAME

INSIDE VIEW OF DOOR

WIRE GLASS

5' 6" DIA.

4'6" DIA.

42"

1/8" HARD-PRESSED BOARD

DOOR FRAME

4" OUTER LEDGE

8" INNER SHELF

1/8" HARD-PRESSED BOARD

3/16" STEEL PLATE

3/16" X 1"

1/2" BOLT

30"

2"X3"

2"X4"

GROOVED

3/4" HALF-ROUND MOLDING

12" BALLOON WHEEL—3/4" C.R.S. AXLE, ROLLER BEARINGS

J-BOLT HOLDS AXLE

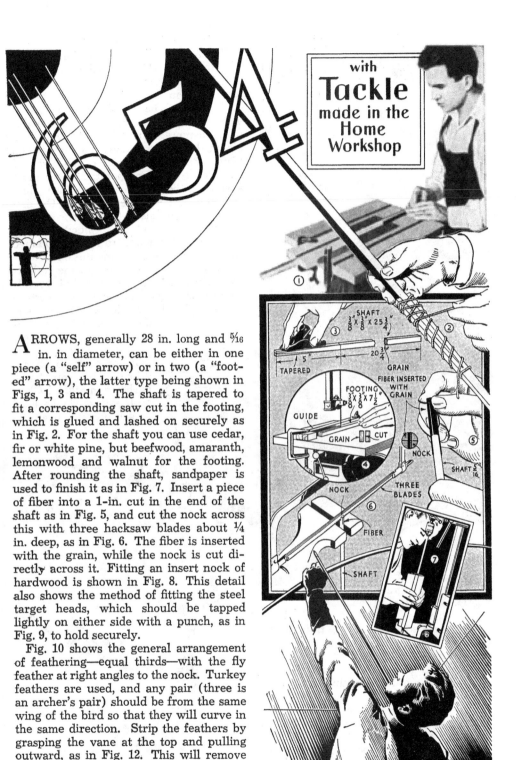

with **Tackle** made in the Home Workshop

ARROWS, generally 28 in. long and 5/16 in. in diameter, can be either in one piece (a "self" arrow) or in two (a "footed" arrow), the latter type being shown in Figs, 1, 3 and 4. The shaft is tapered to fit a corresponding saw cut in the footing, which is glued and lashed on securely as in Fig. 2. For the shaft you can use cedar, fir or white pine, but beefwood, amaranth, lemonwood and walnut for the footing. After rounding the shaft, sandpaper is used to finish it as in Fig. 7. Insert a piece of fiber into a 1-in. cut in the end of the shaft as in Fig. 5, and cut the nock across this with three hacksaw blades about ¼ in. deep, as in Fig. 6. The fiber is inserted with the grain, while the nock is cut directly across it. Fitting an insert nock of hardwood is shown in Fig. 8. This detail also shows the method of fitting the steel target heads, which should be tapped lightly on either side with a punch, as in Fig. 9, to hold securely.

Fig. 10 shows the general arrangement of feathering—equal thirds—with the fly feather at right angles to the nock. Turkey feathers are used, and any pair (three is an archer's pair) should be from the same wing of the bird so that they will curve in the same direction. Strip the feathers by grasping the vane at the top and pulling outward, as in Fig. 12. This will remove the vane from the rib neatly, a thin slice of the rib tegument remaining attached.

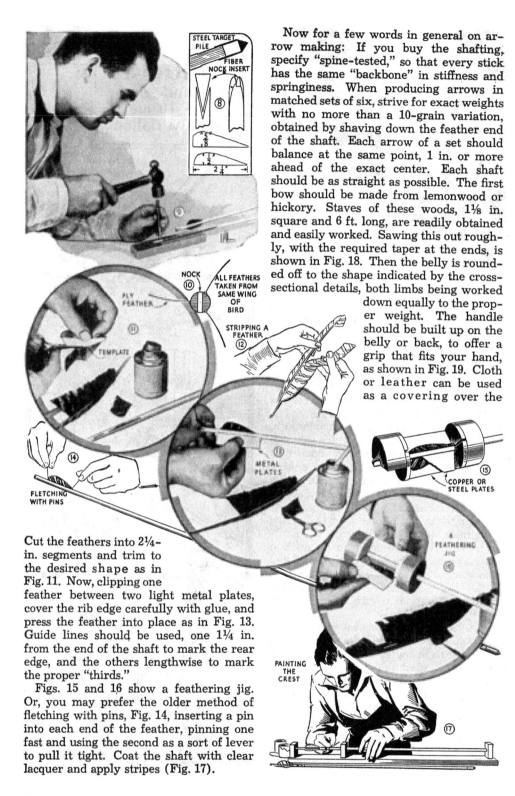

Now for a few words in general on arrow making: If you buy the shafting, specify "spine-tested," so that every stick has the same "backbone" in stiffness and springiness. When producing arrows in matched sets of six, strive for exact weights with no more than a 10-grain variation, obtained by shaving down the feather end of the shaft. Each arrow of a set should balance at the same point, 1 in. or more ahead of the exact center. Each shaft should be as straight as possible. The first bow should be made from lemonwood or hickory. Staves of these woods, 1⅛ in. square and 6 ft. long, are readily obtained and easily worked. Sawing this out roughly, with the required taper at the ends, is shown in Fig. 18. Then the belly is rounded off to the shape indicated by the cross-sectional details, both limbs being worked down equally to the proper weight. The handle should be built up on the belly or back, to offer a grip that fits your hand, as shown in Fig. 19. Cloth or leather can be used as a covering over the

Cut the feathers into 2¼-in. segments and trim to the desired shape as in Fig. 11. Now, clipping one feather between two light metal plates, cover the rib edge carefully with glue, and press the feather into place as in Fig. 13. Guide lines should be used, one 1¼ in. from the end of the shaft to mark the rear edge, and the others lengthwise to mark the proper "thirds."

Figs. 15 and 16 show a feathering jig. Or, you may prefer the older method of fletching with pins, Fig. 14, inserting a pin into each end of the feather, pinning one fast and using the second as a sort of lever to pull it tight. Coat the shaft with clear lacquer and apply stripes (Fig. 17).

shimmed-up handle. Fig. 20 shows how the nocks are cut in at each end of the bow. Use a round file for this, cutting in on the belly and sides of the bow, but not on the back except where the cut comes down at the edges. Horn racks can be fitted if desired, in which case you should work the wood down carefully to make a good fit.

Much has been said about laying up bow strings from so and so many strands of linen thread for each pound of weight. For average use you will find that the better grade of four-strand upholsterer's twine will do quite nicely. Eyes can be spliced into one or both

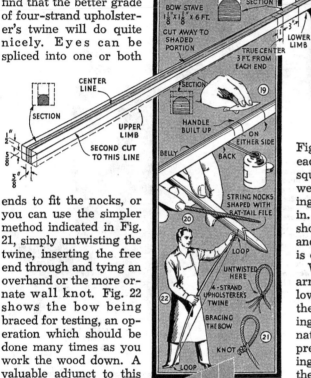

ends to fit the nocks, or you can use the simpler method indicated in Fig. 21, simply untwisting the twine, inserting the free end through and tying an overhand or the more ornate wall knot. Fig. 22 shows the bow being braced for testing, an operation which should be done many times as you work the wood down. A valuable adjunct to this is the "tillering" process,

Fig. 23, which checks the bend of each limb by means of the ruled squares on the walls, while the weight of the bow is read by pulling the bowstring the required 28 in. and reading the scale. Fig. 24 shows the various parts of a bow and the position where the arrow is engaged.

When shooting with a bow and arrow one must learn to make allowance for "windage," that is, the strength of the wind throwing the arrow off its course, which naturally varies. With customary precautions observed when shooting, you will find archery one of the few outdoor sports that gives you fresh air without strenuous exercise. The twang of the string and the "pluck" of the arrow, when it hits the mark, have a fascination and you can be assured that you will develop just as much skill with a homemade outfit, provided it is carefully and accurately made, as you will with expensive equipment that is purchased.

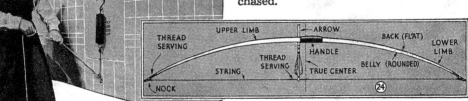

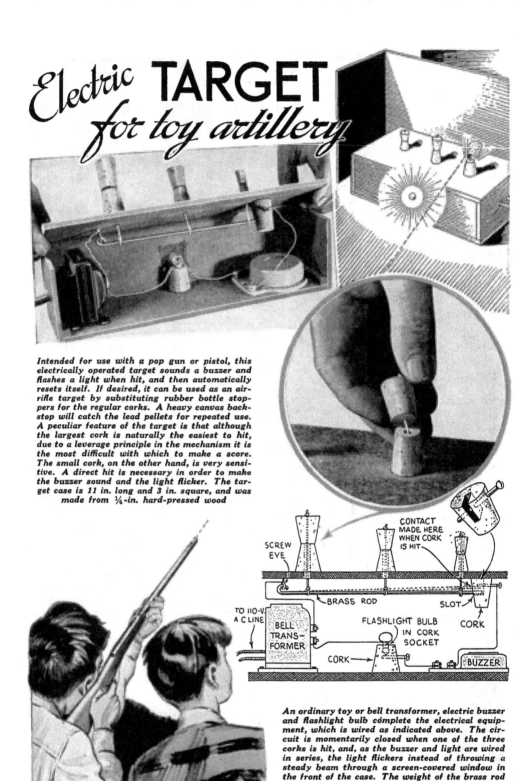

Electric TARGET
for toy artillery

Intended for use with a pop gun or pistol, this electrically operated target sounds a buzzer and flashes a light when hit, and then automatically resets itself. If desired, it can be used as an airrifle target by substituting rubber bottle stoppers for the regular corks. A heavy canvas backstop will catch the lead pellets for repeated use. A peculiar feature of the target is that although the largest cork is naturally the easiest to hit, due to a leverage principle in the mechanism it is the most difficult with which to make a score. The small cork, on the other hand, is very sensitive. A direct hit is necessary in order to make the buzzer sound and the light flicker. The target case is 11 in. long and 3 in. square, and was made from ¼-in. hard-pressed wood

CONTACT MADE HERE WHEN CORK IS HIT

SCREW EYE

TO 110-V. A C LINE

BELL TRANSFORMER

BRASS ROD

FLASHLIGHT BULB IN CORK SOCKET

SLOT

CORK

CORK

BUZZER

An ordinary toy or bell transformer, electric buzzer and flashlight bulb complete the electrical equipment, which is wired as indicated above. The circuit is momentarily closed when one of the three corks is hit, and, as the buzzer and light are wired in series, the light flickers instead of throwing a steady beam through a screen-covered window in the front of the case. The weight of the brass rod returns the corks to their positions after each hit

CAMEL DERBY
interests ~ ~ ~
YOUNG *and* OLD

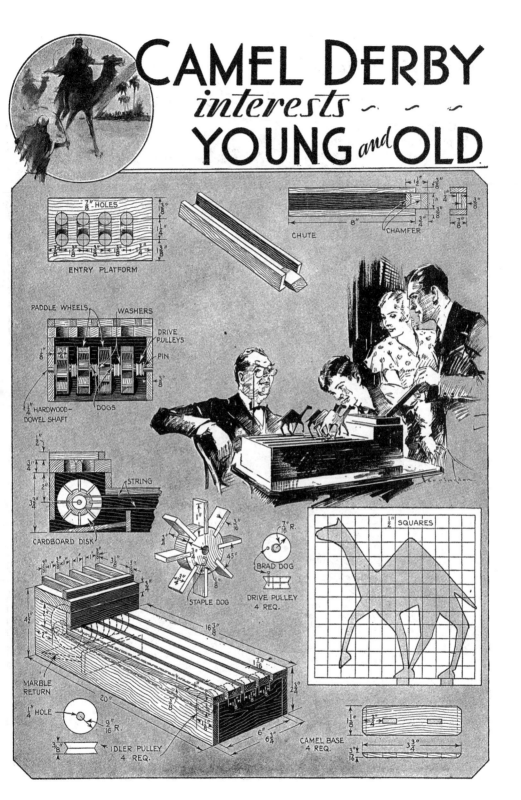

⅞" HOLES

ENTRY PLATFORM

CHUTE

CHAMFER

PADDLE WHEELS   WASHERS

DRIVE PULLEYS

PIN

¼" HARDWOOD-DOWEL SHAFT

DOGS

STRING

CARDBOARD DISK

BRAD DOG

STAPLE DOG

DRIVE PULLEY 4 REQ.

½" SQUARES

MARBLE RETURN

¼" HOLE

9/16" R.

IDLER PULLEY 4 REQ.

16¾"

20"

6"

6¾"

CAMEL BASE 4 REQ.

3¾"

"Steeplechase" in the garden playground

YOUNG jockeys will get plenty of action on this merry-go-round as their steeds take the hurdles. A mere path of hard-packed soil with a little hummock or two forms the circular race track. The hummocks should be on opposite sides so that the effort of pushing one horse up the incline is counterbalanced by its mate coming down the opposite one. The center post is creosoted thoroughly and is set deeply in the ground. As the axis is self-oiling the device will be easy to turn.

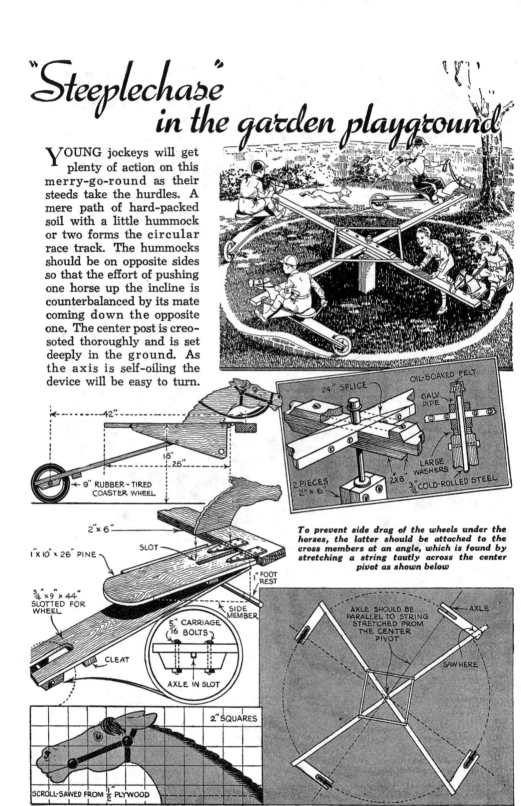

24" SPLICE

OIL-SOAKED FELT

GALV. PIPE

2 PIECES 2" x 6"

2 x 6"

LARGE WASHERS

3/4" COLD-ROLLED STEEL

To prevent side drag of the wheels under the horses, the latter should be attached to the cross members at an angle, which is found by stretching a string tautly across the center pivot as shown below

42"

18"

26"

9" RUBBER-TIRED COASTER WHEEL

2" x 6"

SLOT

1" x 10" x 26" PINE

3/4" x 9" x 44" SLOTTED FOR WHEEL

1" FOOT REST

SIDE MEMBER

5/16" CARRIAGE BOLTS

CLEAT

AXLE IN SLOT

2" SQUARES

AXLE SHOULD BE PARALLEL TO STRING STRETCHED FROM THE CENTER PIVOT

AXLE

SAW HERE

SCROLL-SAWED FROM 1/2" PLYWOOD

The RACING GREYHOUNDS

HERE is a fascinating party game which is of interest to both young and old. It consists of an inclined board having a number of tracks in which miniature greyhounds are sent scooting along in a rather erratic and uncertain way, Figs. 1 and 2. The motive force is supplied by a small motor-driven paddle wheel, which bats golf balls with varying force against the blocks on which the dogs are mounted. By carefully examining the drawings that show the constructional details of this game, you will soon get an accurate idea of just how the mechanism works and how the various parts are assembled.

Strips of ¼-in. plywood are used to divide the top into eight 2-in. lanes in which the smooth blocks that hold the dogs are placed. The three-sided paddle wheel at the lower end of the table should be made of hard maple, and should travel at a speed of from 800 to 1,200 r.p.m. Care must be taken to have the paddle wheel well balanced in order to prevent undue vibration. Almost any small motor will serve to supply the necessary power, and a snap or toggle switch is placed at a convenient position as shown in the drawing.

When playing the game, the first dog that reaches the upper end of the track wins the race. The ball that has been striking it, and is correspondingly numbered, then falls through a hole at the end

of the track, into a return trough which leads to a cup just below the starting point. The frame for the table and the return trough are shown in Fig. 4. Each track, of course, has a hole at its upper end, and in order to prevent any other ball than the winner's from getting into the return trough, a wooden stop is placed directly underneath the row of holes. The stop consists of two pieces of ¼-in. plywood assembled as shown in a detail of Fig. 3, and pivoted at each end. As soon as a ball drops on the horizontal part, the stop moves over to close the row of holes, pre-

119

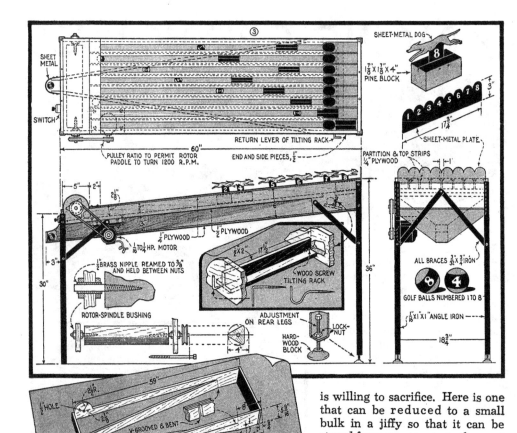

SHEET-METAL DOG

$1\frac{7}{8}" \times 1\frac{7}{8}" \times 4"$ PINE BLOCK

SHEET METAL

SWITCH

RETURN LEVER OF TILTING RACK

60"

PULLEY RATIO TO PERMIT ROTOR PADDLE TO TURN 1200 R.P.M.

END AND SIDE PIECES, $\frac{1}{2}"$

SHEET-METAL PLATE

$17\frac{3}{4}"$

3"

PARTITION & TOP STRIPS $\frac{1}{4}"$ PLYWOOD

5" 2"

$2\frac{1}{8}"$

$\frac{1}{4}"$ PLYWOOD

$\frac{1}{2}"$ PLYWOOD

36"

3"

$\frac{1}{16}$ TO $\frac{1}{4}$ H.P. MOTOR

$\frac{1}{2}"$ BRASS NIPPLE REAMED TO $\frac{3}{8}"$ AND HELD BETWEEN NUTS

$\frac{1}{2}" \times 2"$

$11\frac{1}{2}"$

WOOD SCREW TILTING RACK

ALL BRACES $\frac{3}{32}" \times \frac{3}{4}"$ IRON

30"

ROTOR-SPINDLE BUSHING

ADJUSTMENT ON REAR LEGS

LOCK-NUT

HARD-WOOD BLOCK

GOLF BALLS NUMBERED 1 TO 8

$\frac{1}{8}" \times 1" \times 1"$ ANGLE IRON

4"

$18\frac{3}{4}"$

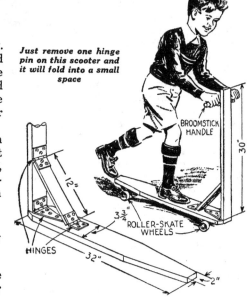

59"

$\frac{1}{2}"$ HOLE

$2\frac{5}{8}$ R.

$2\frac{1}{8}"$

V-GROOVED & BENT

$2\frac{1}{2}"$

66"

is willing to sacrifice. Here is one that can be reduced to a small bulk in a jiffy so that it can be stored from one season to the next or squeezed into a small corner when not in use.

venting any more balls from entering. When a race is finished the motor is turned off, the dogs are all pulled down to the starting position with the balls behind them, the stop is moved over to open the holes and the motor is turned on again for the next race.

It is best to inclose the paddle wheel in a sheet-metal shield. Also, it is convenient to make the legs collapsible, and therefore, angle iron may be used to advantage, rigidity being obtained by means of flat-iron corner braces.

Just remove one hinge pin on this scooter and it will fold into a small space

BROOMSTICK HANDLE

30"

12"

$3\frac{3}{4}"$

ROLLER-SKATE WHEELS

HINGES

32"

2"

Child's Scooter Folds Compactly for Storage

Coasters and scooters often take up more space than the average apartment dweller

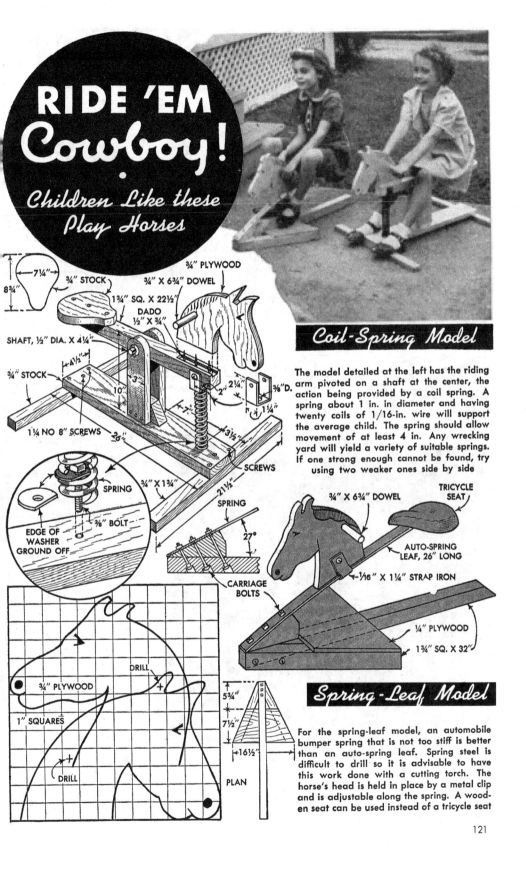

RIDE 'EM Cowboy!

Children Like these Play Horses

¾" PLYWOOD
¾" STOCK
¾" X 6¾" DOWEL
7¼"
8¾"
1¾" SQ. X 22½"
DADO ½" X ¾"
SHAFT, ½" DIA. X 4¼"
¾" STOCK
4½"
3"
10"
2" 2¼"
⅜"D.
1¼"
7"
1¼ NO 8" SCREWS
26"
3½"
SCREWS
SPRING
¾" X 1¾"
21½"
SPRING
EDGE OF WASHER GROUND OFF
⅜" BOLT
27°
CARRIAGE BOLTS
¾" PLYWOOD
1" SQUARES
DRILL
DRILL
5¾"
7½"
16½"
PLAN

Coil-Spring Model

The model detailed at the left has the riding arm pivoted on a shaft at the center, the action being provided by a coil spring. A spring about 1 in. in diameter and having twenty coils of 1/16-in. wire will support the average child. The spring should allow movement of at least 4 in. Any wrecking yard will yield a variety of suitable springs. If one strong enough cannot be found, try using two weaker ones side by side

¾" X 6¾" DOWEL
TRICYCLE SEAT
AUTO-SPRING LEAF, 26" LONG
1/16" X 1¼" STRAP IRON
¼" PLYWOOD
1¾" SQ. X 32"

Spring-Leaf Model

For the spring-leaf model, an automobile bumper spring that is not too stiff is better than an auto-spring leaf. Spring steel is difficult to drill so it is advisable to have this work done with a cutting torch. The horse's head is held in place by a metal clip and is adjustable along the spring. A wooden seat can be used instead of a tricycle seat

121

PLAYING GOLF

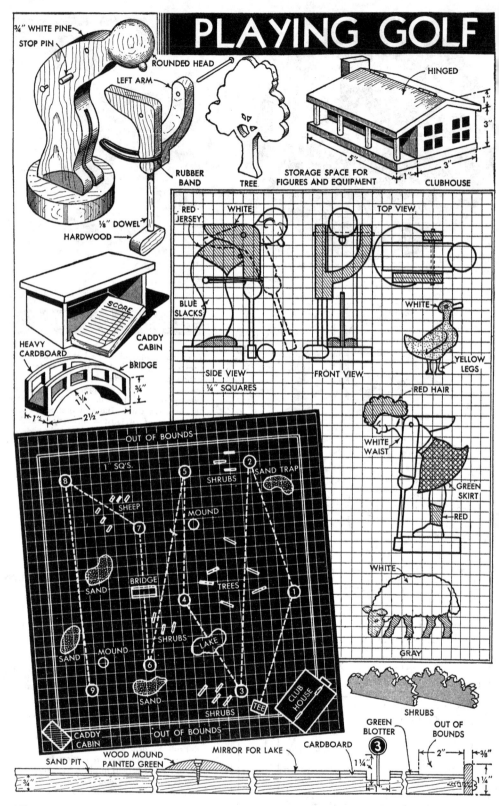

¾" WHITE PINE

STOP PIN

ROUNDED HEAD

LEFT ARM

RUBBER BAND

TREE

STORAGE SPACE FOR FIGURES AND EQUIPMENT

HINGED

1"

3"

5"

3"

1"

CLUBHOUSE

⅛" DOWEL

HARDWOOD

SCORE

CADDY CABIN

HEAVY CARDBOARD

BRIDGE

¾"

1¼"

1"

2½"

RED JERSEY

WHITE

TOP VIEW

BLUE SLACKS

WHITE

YELLOW LEGS

SIDE VIEW

¼" SQUARES

FRONT VIEW

RED HAIR

WHITE WAIST

GREEN SKIRT

RED

OUT OF BOUNDS

1' SQ'S.

SHRUBS

SAND TRAP

8

5

2

SHEEP

MOUND

7

SAND

BRIDGE

TREES

4

1

SHRUBS

LAKE

SAND

MOUND

6

3

9

SAND

SHRUBS

TEE

CLUB HOUSE

CADDY CABIN

OUT OF BOUNDS

WHITE

GRAY

SHRUBS

GREEN BLOTTER

3

OUT OF BOUNDS

2"

⅜"

SAND PIT

WOOD MOUND PAINTED GREEN

MIRROR FOR LAKE

CARDBOARD

1¼"

1¼"

¾"

on a Card Table

Miniature nine-hole course entertains young and old; takes little storage space

MARBLE

HOW GOLFER IS WORKED

MANY hazards in this novel table-top golf course make hole-in-one shots almost as difficult and exciting to score as in the real game. It is played according to standard rules, using a small marble for a golf ball, which is driven by a club held by a "golfer" and manipulated by a player. The course is built on a wooden base to fit the top of a card table and has a hinged-roof clubhouse in which playing equipment is kept when the game is stored away. If plywood can not be had, any ¾-in. scrap wood, glued edgewise, will do for the base, as it is covered with heavy cardboard, such as sign-writer's stock. Glue and tack this to the base and lay out the nine holes on it according to the plan view. Each hole is bored ¼ in. deep with a sharp 1-in. bit, after which the "mirror" lake and "sand-paper" traps are set-in flush. The strip around the edge of the base can extend below the edge also to keep it from shifting on the table. Green desk-blotter stock is used for the fairways and greens and is cut to leave a 2-in. out-of-bounds margin all around. Use rubber cement, or glue, sparingly, to stick it to the cardboard, then cut the holes neatly with a razor blade and give the lake an irregular shoreline.

Both man and woman golfer are made the same way, the right arm of each extending to provide a lever to swing the club. In use, the golfer is held down with the thumb and second finger while the forefinger depresses the lever, pushing the ball rather than striking it. A rubber band, stretched from the arm to a nail in the body, improves control in putting. Make two of each golfer for a foursome and paint each differently for identification. Scroll-saw the trees, shrubs, sheep and geese from ¼-in. wood, and paint the caddy cabin and clubhouse white with red roofs. Tee markers are metal disks soldered to wires.

SHUFFLEBOARD COURT
for the Basement Game Room

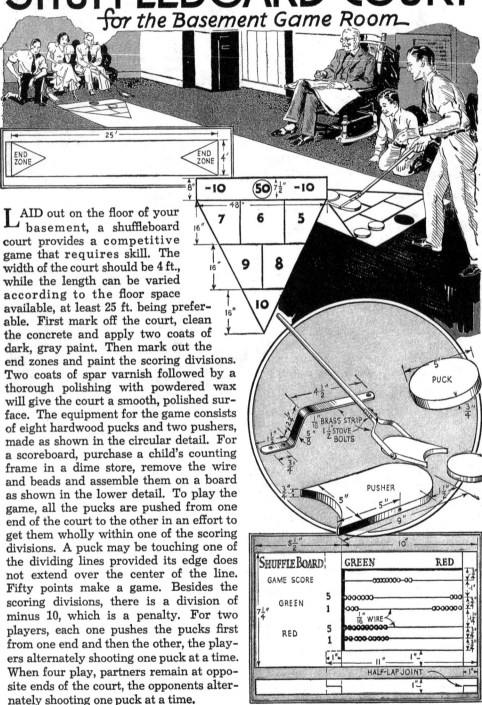

L AID out on the floor of your basement, a shuffleboard court provides a competitive game that requires skill. The width of the court should be 4 ft., while the length can be varied according to the floor space available, at least 25 ft. being preferable. First mark off the court, clean the concrete and apply two coats of dark, gray paint. Then mark out the end zones and paint the scoring divisions. Two coats of spar varnish followed by a thorough polishing with powdered wax will give the court a smooth, polished surface. The equipment for the game consists of eight hardwood pucks and two pushers, made as shown in the circular detail. For a scoreboard, purchase a child's counting frame in a dime store, remove the wire and beads and assemble them on a board as shown in the lower detail. To play the game, all the pucks are pushed from one end of the court to the other in an effort to get them wholly within one of the scoring divisions. A puck may be touching one of the dividing lines provided its edge does not extend over the center of the line. Fifty points make a game. Besides the scoring divisions, there is a division of minus 10, which is a penalty. For two players, each one pushes the pucks first from one end and then the other, the players alternately shooting one puck at a time. When four play, partners remain at opposite ends of the court, the opponents alternately shooting one puck at a time.

"Ocean Roll" MERRY-GO-ROUND

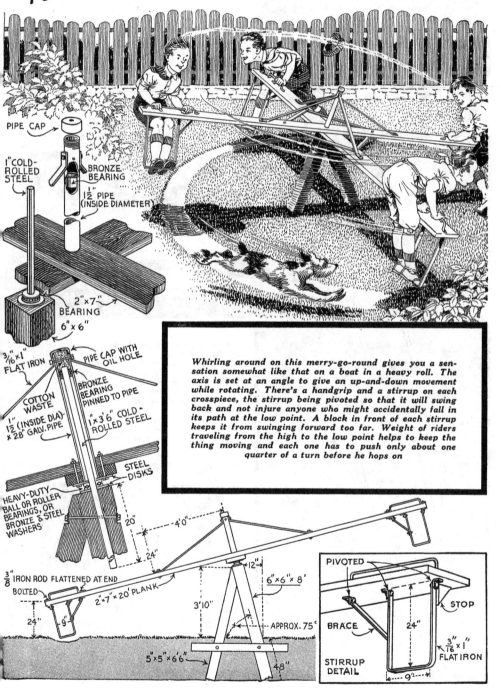

PIPE CAP

1" COLD-ROLLED STEEL

BRONZE BEARING

1½" PIPE (INSIDE DIAMETER)

2"×7" BEARING

6"×6"

3/16"×1" FLAT IRON

PIPE CAP WITH OIL HOLE

COTTON WASTE

BRONZE BEARING PINNED TO PIPE

1" (INSIDE DIA)
1½" × 28" GALV. PIPE

1"×3'6" COLD-ROLLED STEEL

STEEL DISKS

HEAVY-DUTY BALL OR ROLLER BEARINGS, OR BRONZE & STEEL WASHERS

3/8" IRON ROD FLATTENED AT END

BOLTED

2"×7"×20' PLANK

24"

9"

20"

40"

24"

12"

6"×6"×8'

3'10"

APPROX. 75°

5"×5"×6'6"

48"

Whirling around on this merry-go-round gives you a sensation somewhat like that on a boat in a heavy roll. The axis is set at an angle to give an up-and-down movement while rotating. There's a handgrip and a stirrup on each crosspiece, the stirrup being pivoted so that it will swing back and not injure anyone who might accidentally fall in its path at the low point. A block in front of each stirrup keeps it from swinging forward too far. Weight of riders traveling from the high to the low point helps to keep the thing moving and each one has to push only about one quarter of a turn before he hops on

PIVOTED

STOP

BRACE

24"

3/16"×1" FLAT IRON

STIRRUP DETAIL

9"

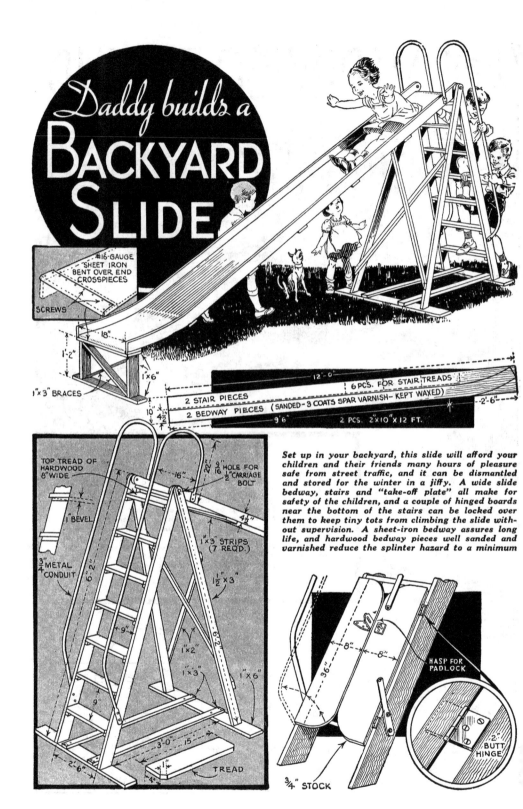

Daddy builds a BACKYARD SLIDE

#16-GAUGE SHEET IRON BENT OVER END CROSSPIECES

SCREWS

18"

1'-2"

1"×6"

1"×3" BRACES

10"

4½"

12'-0"

6 PCS. FOR STAIR TREADS

2 STAIR PIECES

2 BEDWAY PIECES (SANDED-3 COATS SPAR VARNISH- KEPT WAXED)

9'6"

2 PCS. 2"×10"×12 FT.

2'-6"

TOP TREAD OF HARDWOOD 8" WIDE

16"

22"

9/16" HOLE FOR ½" CARRIAGE BOLT

1" BEVEL

4½"

¾" METAL CONDUIT

6'-2"

1"×3" STRIPS (7 REQD.)

1½"×3"

9"

6'-2"

1"×2"

9"

1"×3"

1"×6"

3'-0"

15"

2'-6"

4"

TREAD

Set up in your backyard, this slide will afford your children and their friends many hours of pleasure safe from street traffic, and it can be dismantled and stored for the winter in a jiffy. A wide slide bedway, stairs and "take-off plate" all make for safety of the children, and a couple of hinged boards near the bottom of the stairs can be locked over them to keep tiny tots from climbing the slide without supervision. A sheet-iron bedway assures long life, and hardwood bedway pieces well sanded and varnished reduce the splinter hazard to a minimum

8"

8"

36"

HASP FOR PADLOCK

2"

BUTT HINGE

¾" STOCK

Simple PARTY TRICKS
anyone can do

WHEN the spirit of the party seems to lag, and you're the host, just start things going again with a few simple tricks that can be performed with props available in any home, such as matches, coins, tumblers and paper.

There's the trick of the suspended egg, Fig. 1. Seemingly it defies natural laws by sinking halfway in a jar of water, and going no farther. The reason for this is that there are two liquids in the glass, one on top of the other, care having been taken to prevent them from being mixed. The lower liquid is saturated salt water or brine on which the egg will

FRESH WATER

PAPER DISK

BRINE

THE SUSPENDED EGG

PUZZLING MATCH TRICKS

WHAT HOLDS THE KNIFE?

float (rock salt is used as it does not leave the water milky). The upper liquid is ordinary water in which the egg will sink. After the salt water has been poured into the jar, a paper disk is placed on its surface and the water is added carefully with a spoon or siphon. Then the disk is removed, and the trick may be performed. You announce to the guests that you will cause the egg to submerge in this liquid and that it will come to rest about half way down the jar. Someone is very likely to take issue with you, but when you drop the egg in the jar that is just what happens.

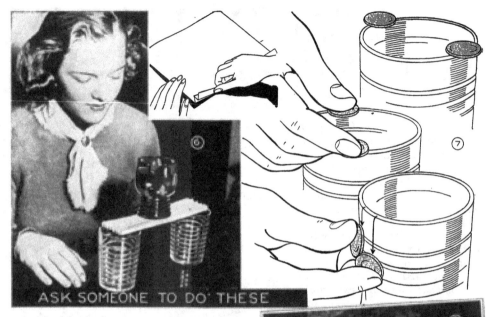

ASK SOMEONE TO DO THESE

Then, a couple of match tricks: The first one involves causing a match to stand unsupported on a piece of wood. Lean the match against a cup, head down on a piece of scrap wood, as shown in Fig. 2. Ignite the head and then blow out the flame quickly. The head will "fuse" to the board sufficiently to hold it in place as in Fig. 3. In the second trick, Fig. 4, you split a match in half and ask someone to drop it in such a way that it will remain on edge. Of course, there's only one way to do it and that involves breaking the match at the center to form a vee.

Another trick, which is simply an illusion, is shown in Fig. 5. It looks as if the knife is glued to the palm of the hand, but the guests don't see the index finger of the right hand, which holds the knife. To all appearances the right hand is grasping the left wrist, and one doesn't pause to count the number of fingers visible.

Now, ask someone to lay a piece of writing paper across a couple of glass tumblers to support a third one partly filled with water, which, of course, seems impossible at first thought. The secret is to pleat the paper by folding it as in Fig. 6 and it will sustain considerable weight before buckling.

The upper detail of Fig. 7 shows two coins balanced on the edge of a tumbler opposite each other. The idea is to remove

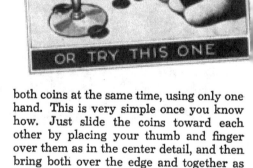

OR TRY THIS ONE

both coins at the same time, using only one hand. This is very simple once you know how. Just slide the coins toward each other by placing your thumb and finger over them as in the center detail, and then bring both over the edge and together as indicated by the arrows in the third detail.

For another coin trick, support a tumbler of water on two nickels under the base, with a penny placed midway between them. Ask someone to remove the penny without touching the glass or nickels. The penny can't be blown out. To do the trick, the setup is arranged squarely with the weave of the tablecloth. Then by repeatedly scratching the cloth with your fingernail as in Fig. 8, the penny will be coaxed out from under the glass.

This Disappearing Coin Trick Is a Real Poser

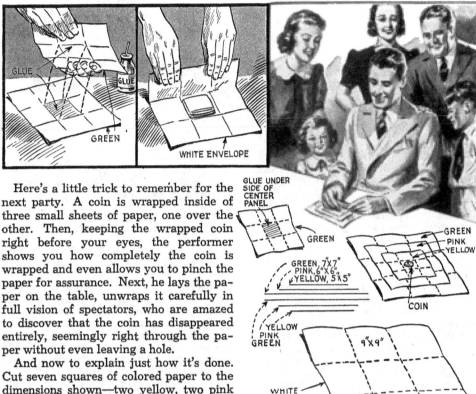

Here's a little trick to remember for the next party. A coin is wrapped inside of three small sheets of paper, one over the other. Then, keeping the wrapped coin right before your eyes, the performer shows you how completely the coin is wrapped and even allows you to pinch the paper for assurance. Next, he lays the paper on the table, unwraps it carefully in full vision of spectators, who are amazed to discover that the coin has disappeared entirely, seemingly right through the paper without even leaving a hole.

And now to explain just how it's done. Cut seven squares of colored paper to the dimensions shown—two yellow, two pink and two green; the largest and last one being white paper. Crease the sheets to fold as indicated by the dotted lines, place the two green sheets back to back and stick the center panels together with glue. Place the green sheets on the table with one pink and one yellow sheet on top, and fold each envelope, starting with the yellow one which should be inclosed in the pink one, and so on. When the folds are completed, reverse the packet so that the unfolded green sheet is uppermost and repeat the process. You now have two packets of folded envelopes but the green ones are glued together through the center panels so that the assembly appears as one package. With this inclosed in the white envelope you are ready for the performance. Placing the packet on the table, you borrow a coin. Ask the donor to observe the date so that when you return it he will see it is the same coin.

Unwrapping the envelopes, and leaving them in the order shown, place the coin in the center of the smallest envelope and re-fold them separately as before, but, before finishing by inclosing in the white envelope, give the green packet an extra turn which will bring the empty assembly of envelopes uppermost. This extra flip of the package will not be noticed by the spectators as your folding is accomplished by turning each envelope over in its turn. Now unfold the sheets. The last and yellow envelope will be found empty. To make the coin re-appear, simply re-fold the envelopes and repeat the turning of the packet after the green one is closed.

—G. E. Hendrickson, Argyle, Wis.

❡A quickly vanishing red ink can be made by dissolving a small quantity of phenolphthalein in strong ammonia. Writing done with this ink disappears a short time after it has been exposed to the air.

Ring-and-Yoke Puzzle to Tax Your Patience

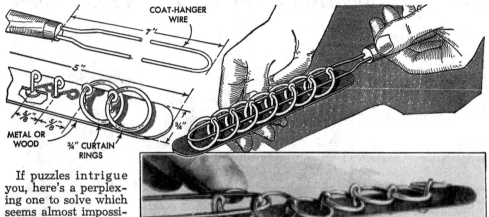

If puzzles intrigue you, here's a perplexing one to solve which seems almost impossible until you know the solution. It consists of seven curtain rings attached to a wood or metal strip through which a wire yoke is threaded as shown—the problem being to slip the yoke from the rings. Either cotter keys or soft-wire nails through oversize holes can be used to attach the rings loosely to the strip. To solve the puzzle, pass the first ring up over the end which is farthest from the handle and down through the loop of the yoke. This will enable you to slide the third ring forward, up and down through in the same way as the first. It will help you in working the puzzle to remember that a ring can be removed only when the ring preceding it is in place. In continuing, replace the first ring by sliding it up through the loop and over the end, just the reverse of the way in which it is removed, and then slip one and two down

through the loop together. This permits sliding ring five forward, over and through, after which one and two are replaced by sliding them together up through the loop and over the end. Next, remove the first ring, replace the third, replace one, remove one and two, remove four, replace one and two, remove one, remove three, replace one and then remove one and two. This permits the seventh or last ring to be slipped through. Since ring five must be replaced before ring six can be removed, you must repeat the steps to replace five; that is, one and two must be slipped on the yoke, then ring one removed so that ring three can be replaced. This procedure is repeated in a similar manner until the yoke is free.

Checkers Played With Marbles on a Book-Shaped Board

You can keep this checkerboard in a bookcase where it will be inconspicuous and always at hand. Also, it will be handy if you want to play checkers on a train trip because motion of the train will not cause the checkers to slide off the board. This is made of solid wood, and marbles are used instead of regular checkers. When not in use, the marbles are kept in a couple of holes drilled horizontally almost through the board, brass or wood covers being pivoted over the holes to retain the marbles.

To keep the marbles from rolling when playing, shallow depressions in the surface of the board are substituted for the usual squares. You will need twelve marbles each of two colors and six or eight each of a third and fourth color for use as kings. The back side of the board can be finished plain, another game laid out on it, or otherwise treated as desired. In the original board, the book effect was further simulated with a title and scored edges to resemble pages.

Indian Bead Work Is Done on Simple Loom

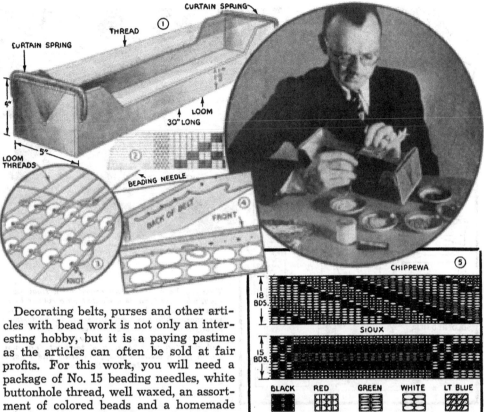

Decorating belts, purses and other articles with bead work is not only an interesting hobby, but it is a paying pastime as the articles can often be sold at fair profits. For this work, you will need a package of No. 15 beading needles, white buttonhole thread, well waxed, an assortment of colored beads and a homemade loom shown in Fig. 1. This can be a cheese box or it may be made up of thin wood. To start weaving, place the beads in small dishes kept close at hand, separating them according to color. Then stretch one thread across the loom for each row of beads on the belt, using three threads for each outside row to strengthen the edges. Now start weaving as shown in Figs. 2 and 3. Tie your weaving thread to the outside loom thread, string the required number of beads and pull them up between the loom threads from the underside. Then run the needle back through the beads from the upper side, repeating this operation until the job is done. In Fig. 4 is shown the method of sewing the beaded work to the belt. Fig. 5 shows Chippewa and Sioux designs with a key to the colors used.—Bob. Hofsinde, Chicago.

❡Fingernail polish will keep pyro film developer from staining the nails.

Hat Held Tightly on Wall by Spring Hook

Instead of hanging your hat on a nail or hook in a closet, where it is often knocked down, try the hanger shown. It is a piece of clock or phonograph spring drilled and screwed to the wall, first rounding the lower end and smoothing the edges with a file. The brim of the hat is slipped between the spring and the wall where it is held tightly. If necessary, use metal lacquer on the springs to prevent rust.

PIECE OF PHONOGRAPH SPRING

Midget Oarsman Works This Toy Rowboat

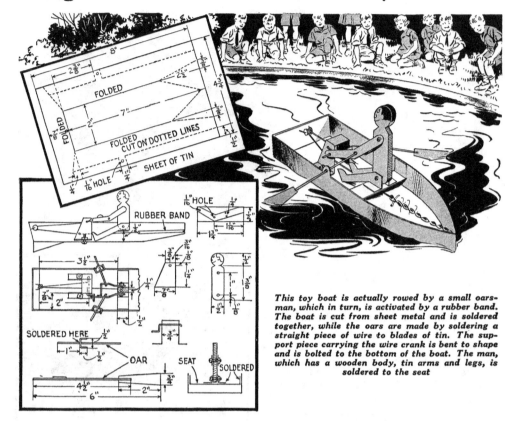

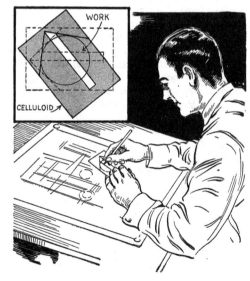

This toy boat is actually rowed by a small oarsman, which in turn, is activated by a rubber band. The boat is cut from sheet metal and is soldered together, while the oars are made by soldering a straight piece of wire to blades of tin. The support piece carrying the wire crank is bent to shape and is bolted to the bottom of the boat. The man, which has a wooden body, tin arms and legs, is soldered to the seat

Finding the Center of Circles Without Rule or Compass

Finding the center of a circle is easy with this simple instrument. It consists of a rectangular sheet of thin, transparent celluloid on which is drawn a right angle in the position shown. Score the lines and ink them so that they are easily seen. Divide the angle in half, locating two 45° points. Then along a line drawn between the points, cut through the celluloid with a sharp knife, guiding it with a straightedge. Make another cut parallel to the first and cut out the waste, leaving a slot about $5/16$ in. wide. In use, place the instrument over the circle with the right-angle lines tangent to the circle. Then draw a line across the circle, using the long side of the slot as a guide. Shift the instrument 90°, place it in the same relative position and draw a second line which will intersect the first one. The point of intersection is the center of the circle.

"Juggling Cat" Tosses Ball from Paw to Paw

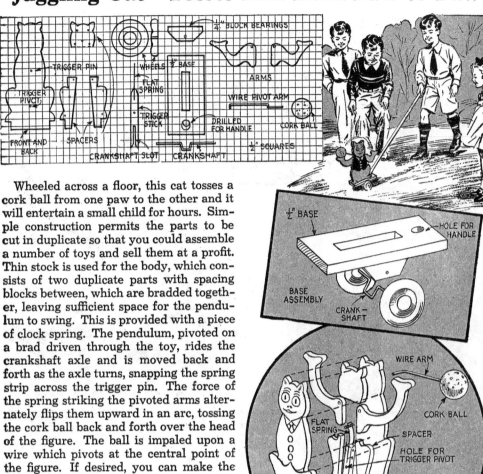

Wheeled across a floor, this cat tosses a cork ball from one paw to the other and it will entertain a small child for hours. Simple construction permits the parts to be cut in duplicate so that you could assemble a number of toys and sell them at a profit. Thin stock is used for the body, which consists of two duplicate parts with spacing blocks between, which are bradded together, leaving sufficient space for the pendulum to swing. This is provided with a piece of clock spring. The pendulum, pivoted on a brad driven through the toy, rides the crankshaft axle and is moved back and forth as the axle turns, snapping the spring strip across the trigger pin. The force of the spring striking the pivoted arms alternately flips them upward in an arc, tossing the cork ball back and forth over the head of the figure. The ball is impaled upon a wire which pivots at the central point of the figure. If desired, you can make the toy to suit the season. A rabbit can be substituted for the cat, and the ball can be replaced with an "egg," to convert the toy into an Easter special.

A Wax Finish on Wood Plates, Spoons and Salad Bowls

Here is an excellent penetrating wax that will give a high luster to natural-finished wood plates, salad bowls, etc., and contains nothing that contaminates or imparts a flavor to the food. It is made by melting pure, white beeswax and stirring in an equal amount of olive oil as the wax cools. The mixture will solidify at room temperature. A lump of it will smooth out under the warmth of the bare hands as it is rubbed on the work with the fingers. Further friction of polishing with a soft cloth makes a perfect spread of the right consistency. The finish is brightened easily without polish and is impervious to finger marks.—H. Thompson, Westfield, N. J.

¶Gauze bandage material provides good facings for sheer wash frocks when the hem has been let down and there is no matching goods. It has the advantage of being pre-shrunk and therefore does not pucker when laundered.

COMPARTMENT FOR BB SHOT

⅜" X 1" X 12"

¼" SPACER PIPES 6½" LONG

2¾"

NAIL

WASHERS

WASHER

FACE UPSIDE DOWN

¼" ROD

TOE-NAILED

2" X 4"

STAKE

36"

19½"

3½"R

12"

9"

2½"R

⅜" X 2"

48"

¾" X 10" X 71" TOP

¾" X 4" X 60"

2" X 4" X 34½"

2" X 4" X 20"

8"

EVERY youngster loves a carnival and dreams of having one right in his own backyard, which is possible with the amusement devices suggested here. All are safe and none of them involves the use of rifles, dangerous electric connections or other hazardous accessories. Inexpensive lumber and old material may be used for the stands, horses and supports, as they are to be painted in bright colors which will hide the defects. Colored bunting or crepe paper also may be used to advantage.

As no carnival would be complete without an "attraction" that tests the skill in throwing a baseball, we start off with the game of "Make Old Sourpuss Smile." A piece of canvas is stretched between poles, as shown in Fig. 2, and a hole about 10 in. in diameter is cut through the canvas with the center just 51 in. above the ground. Behind this opening is placed a rack with the double

in the Backyard

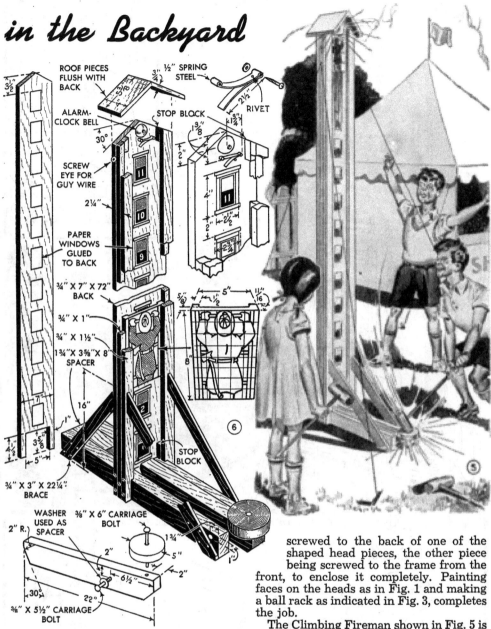

ROOF PIECES FLUSH WITH BACK

½" SPRING STEEL

RIVET

ALARM-CLOCK BELL

STOP BLOCK

SCREW EYE FOR GUY WIRE

2¼"

PAPER WINDOWS GLUED TO BACK

¾" X 7" X 72" BACK

¾" X 1"

¾" X 1½"

1¾" X 3⅝" X 8" SPACER

STOP BLOCK

¾" X 3" X 22¼" BRACE

WASHER USED AS SPACER

⅜" X 6" CARRIAGE BOLT

2" R.

⅜" X 5½" CARRIAGE BOLT

head as detailed in Fig. 4. The device is arranged so that if the ball strikes the scowling face it will swing over and the smiling face will appear behind the opening. The next time it is hit the faces will be reversed again.

The swinging unit consists of two scroll-sawed pieces and a closed frame to contain BB shot, which serves as a weight to keep the unit in a vertical position, the shot rolling from end to end when a head is hit and turned over. The frame is assembled and

screwed to the back of one of the shaped head pieces, the other piece being screwed to the frame from the front, to enclose it completely. Painting faces on the heads as in Fig. 1 and making a ball rack as indicated in Fig. 3, completes the job.

The Climbing Fireman shown in Fig. 5 is the answer to boys who want to show their strength. It consists of a vertical track on which a block, painted to represent a fireman, is made to climb by striking a disk on the end of a treadle with a croquet mallet. This causes the inner end of the treadle to drive the figure up a back board or track, as shown in Fig. 5. Windows, to simulate a skyscraper, are painted or pasted on the board at intervals to indicate how many floors the player has made the fireman climb. If the player succeeds in driving the fireman to the top, a bell rings, indicating

4" SQ'S. ⑦

13" 12"
6"
12"
7"
17½"
11⅛"
17"
19⅛"
72"
12"
3½" X 16"
¾" X 1½"
39⅞"
16"
HALF-LAPPED JOINTS
48"
48"
12"
⑨

⑧

¾" X 1½" X 54"
2"
¼" X 48" X 72" WALLBOARD

5"
1/32 SHEET METAL
5"
1⅜" R.
6"
1½"
2½"
¾"

4½" DIA. HOLE
3⅛"
1/32" X ¾" SHEET METAL
½"
GREEN CELLOPHANE
CONTACT SPRING
⑩

METAL REFLECTOR
2½"
TARGET
SPRING
3-VOLT LAMPS
BATTERY

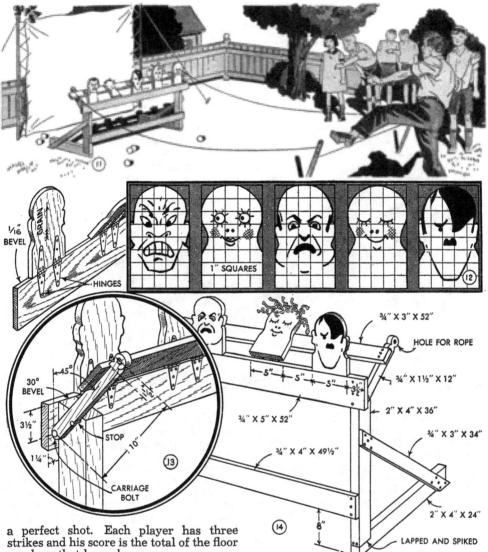

a perfect shot. Each player has three strikes and his score is the total of the floor numbers that he makes.

The treadle is pivoted to a frame consisting of two strong pieces, either solid or built-up stock, which are nailed together with a spacer at the back. The disk or strike plate is made of hardwood and is bolted to the treadle with the grain of the wood running at right angles to the treadle. The back board, shown in Fig. 6, is cut out at the bottom to straddle the treadle frame, which is screwed to it and braced diagonally. Guide strips at the edges form grooves in which the fireman slides, and stop blocks at the top check the figure at this point. The top of the back board is finished off with two pieces to simulate a roof. The figure is recessed at the back to reduce friction and to avoid scraping loose the paper windows. In use, the device is supported further by stakes driven along-

side the treadle frame and by four guy wires.

The Green-Eyed-Buddha Target shown in Fig. 8 has a special appeal for young archers. A medal on the chest has to be hit with a suction-cup arrow. Then the eyes light up green and remain lighted until the target is reset. The target consists of a large figure cut out of wallboard as shown in Fig. 7. Fig. 9 shows a rear view of the target and the wood framework to which the wallboard figure is tacked. Three shelves are provided for batteries, target switch and miniature lamps. Two large 1½-volt dry cells are connected in series to provide current for the 3-volt lamps.

The medal is cut to the shape indicated in Fig. 10. Projections on the lower cor-

137

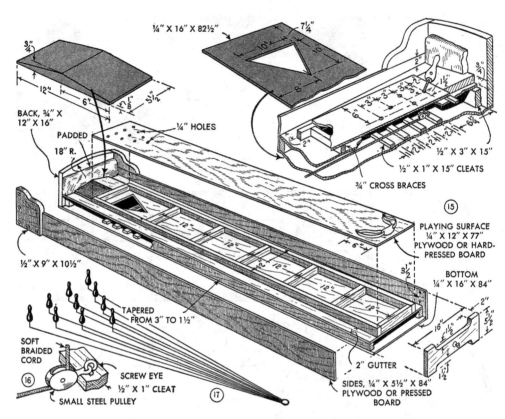

BACK, ¾" X 12" X 16"

PADDED 18" R.

¼" X 16" X 82½"

7¼"

¼" HOLES

½" X 3" X 15"

½" X 1" X 15" CLEATS

¾" CROSS BRACES

(15)

PLAYING SURFACE ¼" X 12" X 77" PLYWOOD OR HARD-PRESSED BOARD

BOTTOM ¼" X 16" X 84"

½" X 9" X 10½"

TAPERED FROM 3" TO 1½"

SOFT BRAIDED CORD

(16)

SCREW EYE ½" X 1" CLEAT

(17)

SMALL STEEL PULLEY

2" GUTTER

SIDES, ¼" X 5½" X 84" PLYWOOD OR PRESSED BOARD

ners are bent so that they fit an iron bracket to which the medal is pivoted loosely enough so that a slight blow will cause it to swing back and make contact with a brass strip. Two wood screws and a machine screw are used to mount the contact strip on a shelf behind the target opening. An additional machine screw or binding post is used to anchor a "pig-tail" connector of flexible wire, which is soldered to the medal. Two miniature sockets for the lamps are screwed to a shelf directly behind the eye holes, which are covered with green Cellophane. The wiring diagram is shown in the lower right-hand detail of Fig. 10.

Man Overboard as shown in Figs. 11 to 14, is a riot of fun for everyone. It is really the old "Doll Rack" in a new form and with a reset arrangement operated by simply pulling a cord. The object of the game is to see how many figures can be knocked over with five baseballs. A canvas backstop is arranged to catch the balls that go wild. Fig. 14 details the rack and Fig. 13 shows the reset arrangement. The designs for the various heads are shown in Fig. 12, and the method of hinging them to a base is shown in the detail at the left. The features are painted on the pieces after they have been band-sawed to shape.

The Catapult Bowling Alley will furnish fun and amusement galore, and is large enough to play a real game involving considerable skill and technique. The game is played essentially the same as on a regulation bowling alley except that the ball is catapulted as shown in Fig. 19 instead of being rolled, and the pins are reset by pulling cords. Scoring is the same as regular bowling, a game consisting of ten frames with only two balls played for each frame. If all the pins are knocked down by the first ball, the score is called a strike and the second ball is not used. A strike is indicated by "X" on your score card, Fig. 20. If some of the pins remain standing, the second ball is played. Should this ball knock down the remaining pins, you have scored a spare, indicated by "/". A strike entitles the player to a score of 10 points plus what is made on the next two balls bowled. A spare entitles the player to 10 points plus the score made on the next ball played. If neither a strike nor a spare is scored in the frame, the total number of pins knocked down are counted as your score. Should a strike be made in the 10th frame, two additional balls are played immediately and the total score determined. A spare entitles the player to one additional ball. Strikes, spares and blows

138

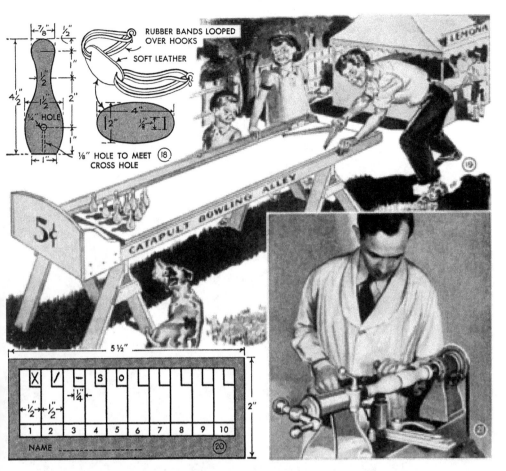

RUBBER BANDS LOOPED OVER HOOKS

SOFT LEATHER

⅛" HOLE TO MEET ⑱ CROSS HOLE

NAME _ _ _ _ _ _ _ _ _ _ ⑳

(neither strike nor spare) are indicated on the score card immediately, but the number of points cannot be indicated until the additional balls have been played in the case of spares and strikes. The score for each frame consists of the points made in that frame plus those made in the previous frame and your final score is the amount shown at the end of the 10th frame.

Fig. 15 shows how the alley is constructed. The ends, spacers and cleats are made of solid wood, and the other parts of plywood or hard-pressed wood. A pad at the end of the alley is used to absorb the force of the ball. A sloping block at the back diverts the ball to one of the gutters, these being slanted toward the front so that the ball will be returned to the player. A 1½-in. billiard ball is used to play the game. Fig. 18 shows a detail of a pin and the catapult sling. Heavy rubber bands are looped through the leather ball holder and secured to two large screw eyes that have been opened just enough to admit the rubber bands. The pins are turned in pairs as in Fig. 21.

Figs. 16 and 17 show the arrangement of the cords and a detail of the small awning pulleys that are used to set the pins from the front of the alley. The cords are strung through holes in the bottoms of the pins, and drawn out through the intersecting side holes for knotting. The cords pass through the holes on the playing surface and through a triangular opening in the gutter floor under the playing surface. Then they are run through the pulleys directly under the holes and are brought out to the front of the alley where they are all tied to a ring. When the pins are all set up there is a slack of about 8 in. in the cords to permit the pins to be knocked down. Soft braided cotton cord about 3/32 in. in diameter is used.

Replacing Motorcycle Chain

When the rear chain of a motorcycle must be removed for cleaning and greasing, it can be replaced on the front sprocket more easily if a length of old chain is attached to the one being removed. This is left hanging around the front sprocket, and used to pull the regular chain into place.